Enriching Christian Doctrine and Character

Fifty-Two Studies

Divided into Four Themes

God the Father
God the Son
God the Spirit
God's Believers

Michael J. Akers, Ph.D.

authorHOUSE®

AuthorHouse™
1663 Liberty Drive, Suite 200
Bloomington, IN 47403
www.authorhouse.com
Phone: 1-800-839-8640

First published by AuthorHouse   3/2/2009

ISBN: 978-1-4389-4891-1 (e)
ISBN: 978-1-4389-4890-4 (sc)

Printed in the United States of America
Bloomington, Indiana

This book is printed on acid-free paper.

Purpose

God exists as God the Father, God the Son, and God the Spirit. We are God's people who relate to God in each of these manifestations. I selected 13 key topics that cover basic Biblical doctrine on these four descriptors of whom God is and who we are as His children. My intent was to fill a maximum of two pages for each of fifty-two Biblical topics with sufficient Scripture references to enable the reader to fill an entire week looking up each Scripture and both thinking and learning about what it is being taught.

Each study is a blend of my own learning and selections from books and the internet that I wanted to include. I have done my best to credit others whose writings I have referenced. Also, I have attempted to be accurate in the Scriptures I have chosen to be included. I apologize in advance if there are any mistakes.

Each study also contains questions for discussion somewhere in the text or as a separate list and concludes with at least one memorable quote.

May each person spending time with this material be blessed by what the Holy Spirit does through these words of learning. May you not only learn a great deal, but also apply what you have learned in serving the Lord by serving others.

Michael J. Akers
February 1, 2009

Table of Contents

Study Topics on God the Spirit

Study Topics on God's Believers

Study Topics on God The Father

1. God The Father

When you think of God, do you have a picture in your mind? Describe it.

<u>Biblical names for God</u>
There are 16 different names describing God in Old Testament (O.T.) Scripture, 10 different names in the New Testament (N.T.). Here are the 7 descriptive names of God most often used:

- YAHWEH (YHWH, Jehovah) -- "LORD" (Deut 6:4; Dan 9:14) – Strictly speaking, the only proper name for God. The name is first given to Moses "I Am who I Am" (Exo 3:14).   YHWH is used in O.T. more than any other name for God (6519 times).

- ADONAI-- "Lord" (Gen 15:2; Judges 6:15) – Used in place of YHWH, thought by the Jews to be too sacred to be uttered by sinful men. In the O.T., YHWH is more often used in God's dealings with His people, while Adonai is used when He deals with the Gentiles.

- EI, ELOAH--God "mighty, strong, prominent" (Gen 7:1; Isa 9:6).

- ELOHIM--God "Creator, Mighty and Strong" (Gen 17:7; Jer 31:33) – The plural form of Eloah, accommodates the doctrine of the Trinity. The superlative nature of God's power is evident as God (Elohim) speaks the world into existence (Gen 1:1).

- EL SHADDAI--"God Almighty,""The Mighty One of Jacob" (Gen 49:24; Psalm 132:2, 5) Speaks to God's ultimate power over all.

- THEOS—Greek word for Elohim, used over 1,000 times in N.T.

- ABBA—Aramic word Jesus used, meaning Father. Used 245 times in N.T., 15 in O.T.

<u>God the Father in the Old Testament (1)</u>
- God of mercy (Exo 34:6-7)
- God who establishes and keeps covenants (Gen 9:1; 12:1-3; Exo 19:5-6)
- Redeemer God (Psalm 8:3-4; 18:1-2; Isa 44:6)
- God of refuge (Psalm 27:5; 36:5-9; 46:1; 62:8)
- God of forgiveness (Psalm 51)
- God of goodness (Psalm 146:7-9)
- God of faithfulness (Isaiah 41:9-10; 44:21-22; 45:22)
- God of salvation and vengeance (Isaiah 35:4)
- God of security and protection, our Shepherd (Psalm 23)
- Re-emphasis of a Father God (Deut 32.6; Isa 64:8; Malachi 1:6; 2:10)

<u>God the Father in the New Testament (1)</u>
- Father of all believers (Matt 5:45; 6:6-15; John 1:12-13; Gal 4:5-6; Romans 8:15-16)
- Father revealed through Jesus (John 1:1,14,18; 14:9)
- Father of love (Luke 6:35,36; Luke 15, John 3:16, II Thess 2:16-17)
- Father as a rewarder (Matt 6:20; Heb 11:6)
- Father of 7 spiritual blessings (Eph 1:3-14)
- Father of the least of humankind (Matt 25:40)
- Father of the Second coming (Matt 16:27; 26.64; Rev 6:16)

Main descriptions about the person of God
- **Immanence**—closely related to omnipresence, God is always present within the universe, though distinct from it. God is the sustainer of the universe (Jer 23:23-24; Ps 24; Col 1:17).
- **Omnipresence**-- God is spirit; He has no physical form. He is present everywhere in that everything is immediately in His presence. At the same time He is present everywhere in the universe. No one can hide from Him and nothing escapes His notice (Ps 139:7-12)
- **Omniscience**—God is all-knowing (Psalm 147:5; Rom 11:33; Heb 4:12-13)
- **Omnipotence**—God can do anything within His will. If He says something will happen, it will because He has the power to make it happen. He has the power to grant eternal life to those who believe in Jesus Christ. He has the power to forgive sin (Matt 19:26; Jer 32:17, 27).
- **Other attributes**: **Glorious** (Ps 19:1); **Sovereign** (Ps 46:10); **Holy** (I John 1:5); **Just** (Rom 3:25-26); **Love** (John 1:29; John 3:16; I John 4:7-21); **Comforter** (II Cor 1:3); **Faithful** (Lam 3:22-23); **Unchanging** (Mal 3:6), many others.

How can you be sure that God exists?
Read Psalm 19:1; 24:1; all of 104; Romans 1:20. One of the "toughest" statements you have to defend in your life is: "I believe in God". That is exactly what is required when you read Gen 1:1. God had no beginning. God has no end. You can say "I don't understand that". I don't either. We simply have to believe. We have to rely on faith that what the Bible says in absolute truth.

God's Seven Wonders (2) (To be discussed in subsequent lessons/discussion)
1. God's love
2. That God came to live among us
3. The cross
4. People can be converted
5. God's gifts of peace and joy through Christ
6. God's plan for the future
7. Your and my commitment to Christ

Questions
1. What names or descriptions of God do you like the best?
2. Read Psalm 103 and list all the descriptions of who God is.
3. Read Isaiah 40 and reflect on the incomparable greatness of God
4. What makes God seem the most real to you?
5. In I John 3:1-3, God says that we believers are His children. Discuss the staggering reality of this truth. Also read John 1:12 and use both of these passages to capture fully what it means to be a child of God. How does this truth help you face your life's problems and challenges?
6. The ways that God acts toward us are an obvious guide for how He wants us to act toward others. What godly character can you work on to develop more fully?
7. Discuss this statement: "Life's major pursuit is not knowing self, but knowing God"

Quote
- "If you can understand it, it is not God"--St. Augustine
- "It is quite natural and inevitable that, if you spend 16 hours daily in your waking hours in thinking about the affairs of the world and 5 minutes thinking about God and your soul, no wonder this world seems 200 times more real to you than God"—William Ralph Enge

2. Worship

How do you define "worship"?

Christians understand the need to read the Bible and to spend time in prayer, but many believers don't understand the importance of worship. We can worship the Lord while we're singing, while we're praying, or while we're meditating on God. But too often we sing, pray, and meditate without spending time really worshipping the Lord.

Meaning of Worship

The word "worship" occurs 188 times in the Bible. Over 95% of the time, it is used to translate one of the following four words (1):

1. **Shachah** --make low, bow, prostrate, fall down, reverence.
2. **Seged**--prostrate, pay homage (found only in Dan.—bowing to the golden image; in Isaiah--hand-made idols, and II Kings -- worship of Baal)
3. **Proskunew** --kiss, fawn, prostrate, bow, reverence, honor
4. **Sebomai** --used of Jewish and pagan worship, not Christian.

Some practical illustrations of worship (2)

- Worship is the way we see God's larger purpose for us. A life of worship usually doesn't make media headlines, but even the smallest things done in relation to God are significant because they're part of a grand plan.
- Worship means fully opening your heart to God and expressing your true love and feelings for Him.
- Worship means not just saying the words to a song in church. It means actually meaning them with your heart.

Psalm 100 teaches us about worship (3)

Verse 1 *Make a joyful shout to the LORD, all you lands!*
Who is to worship God? This verse tells us "all you lands." God desires that every believer in every nation spends time worshipping him. That means everyone — no exceptions. What happens when we worship him is that our spirit is being mysteriously fed as we commune with God. As we are blessing the Lord, we are being blessed by the Lord. What is the proper way to worship? This verse tells us to "make a joyful shout". Psalm 46:10 tells us, "Be still, and know that I am God" Psalm 95:6 says, "O come, let us worship and bow down: let us kneel before the LORD our maker." There is no one way to worship God. Do it when you're standing, when you're kneeling, when you're lying on your face before the Lord. Praise him with a shout, with quietness, with clapping, with lifting up of hands. In all things, in all ways, at all times worship the Lord.

Verse 2 *Serve the LORD with gladness; come before His presence with singing.*
When are we to worship God? The first words of this verse say, "Serve the Lord." In our daily walk, when we are at work, at home, or at leisure, we are to serve Him. Also notice that throughout the day we are to serve the Lord with gladness. Serving God is not a drudgery. As we learn to serve God in everything throughout every day, we discover true joy and happiness. When we spend time in prayer, let's not make the mistake of taking all the time to ask for things from God. We need to spend time praising and magnifying God in our hearts. We can also worship the Lord with singing. As we lift up our voice in song to God, we need to allow our heart to worship the Lord. We need to do more than just sing, than just enjoy the music, than just be moved emotionally. We need to allow God's Spirit to fill us with his presence as we focus on the goodness of the Lord. We need to worship our Creator.

Verse 3 *Know that the LORD, He is God; it is He who has made us, and not we ourselves; we are His people and the sheep of His pasture.*

Why we worship him? Because of what he has done for us. This verse starts with the word "know." We worship him because we know these things. God has revealed these truths to us. The word Lord in the Hebrew is *Yahweh*. Yahweh was the name by which God revealed himself to Israel as the covenant-keeper. This Hebrew word for God is *Elohim*. This is the word used for the creator, the ruler of the universe. We worship him because we know that no matter what may happen to us, God is in control of everything. He made us and is continuing to form us. We worship him because we know we are in good hands. We know that he knows exactly what's best for us. He is making us into what he wants us to be. This little phrase "and not we ourselves" reminds us that we didn't save ourselves, but he provided the way. He provided the perfect sacrifice for our sins. Nothing we did made us deserving of his grace. It was his free gift to us.

Verse 4 *Enter into His gates with thanksgiving, and into His courts with praise. Be thankful to Him, and bless His name.*

How we are to worship him? We start by entering his gates —entering into his presence. Leave the cares of this life behind and begin to enter into his presence with worship in our heart. As we begin entering into communion with the Lord, we are overwhelmed with feelings of gratitude. As we praise him in our heart, we think of all the good things God has done for us. As our heart is filled with gratitude to the Lord, we find ourselves entering into his courts. We begin to sense his power and majesty surrounding us. Our heart is filled with praise to our God. He has done so much for us, we can't help but praise him. We become like David who wrote in Psalm 103:1, "Bless the LORD, O my soul: and all that is within me, bless his holy name."

Verse 5

For the LORD is good; his mercy is everlasting, and His truth endures to all generations.

Why we worship him, Part 2? Because of who He is. This verse gives us three attributes of his character that should cause our heart to leap with praise—His goodness, His mercy, and His truth.

Questions
1. What do the following Psalms teach about worship? 8, 42, 95.
2. Why are we to worship God? Discuss Isa 43-44
3. What does it mean to worship God "in spirit and truth" (John 4:24) and "in the Spirit of God and glory in Christ Jesus (Phil 3:3)?
4. Rick Warren's Purpose Driven Life says that our #1 purpose in life is to worship God. You and I were planned for God's pleasure (Isa 61:3), to magnify His glory, to love Him with all of your heart, and to answer the following question: "Who will be the center of my life?" Other questions from Warren:
   a. Where in my daily routine can I become more aware of God's glory? – Rom 11:36
   b. How can I remind myself that life is really about living for God, not myself? – Col 1:16

Quote
➢ "Without worship, we go about miserable." -- A.W. Tozer

3. Seeking God

How do you really seek God? What does "seek" really mean? What are you really expecting to find if you seek God?

Seeking God is a commandment found throughout the Scriptures (112 references in the O.T.; 16 references in the N.T). Seeking God is a discipline that His true followers must do, but what does it really mean (1)?

- Seeking God is the spirit of man longing for fellowship with God (Ps 63:1; Isa 26:9; John 4:23)
- The very purpose of man's existence is to seek God (Acts 17:26-28).
- Seeking God is a commandment and part of the character of a godly person (I Chron 16:10-11)
- Seeking God is not a casual exercise; it requires diligent effort like searching for treasure (Prov 2:1-5). Other descriptions of the effort required to seek God:
  - o Seek His face continually—I Chron 16:11
  - o Seek with all heart and soul—II Chron 15:12; Jer 29:13; Psalm 119:2
  - o Seek Him earnestly—Psalm 63:1
  - o Seek Him first—Matt 6:33, Psalm 27:4
- Failure to seek after God results in spiritual death (Isa 5:13, Hosea 4:6).
- God looks for those who make the effort to seek Him (Psalm 14:2, 53:2; John 4:23)
- God promises that those who diligently seek him shall find him (Deut 4:29-31; Jer 29:11,14; I Chron 28:9; Psalms 9:10; Prov 8:17; Matt 7:7; John 6:37; James 4:8)
- We do not seek Him in vain (Isa 45:19; Mal 3:13-14)

Practically, how do we seek God? Perhaps a study of Daniel 9 can help.

He promises certain blessings and rewards to those who diligently seek Him (Psalm 107:9; Lamentations 3:25; Hebrews 11:6)
1. Joy--Psalms 70:4; 105:3
2. Peace and rest--2 Chron 14:7; 15:12-15
3. Revelation--Jer 33:3
4. Understanding in the ways of God--Prov 28:5
5. Strength--1 Chron 16:11; Psalms 105:4; Isa 40:31; 41:1
6. Prosperity and provision-- 2 Chron 26:5; Psalm 34:9, 10; Matt 6:33
7. Security--Psalm 27:4-5

How do we seek God and what happens when we make the effort? (2)
God rewards those who diligently seek Him. In order to come to God, we must believe this great truth. Confidently acting on our faith and passionately pursuing Him, we will find the God whom we were created to enjoy. He has promised that we will not only find Him, but find in Him all that our hearts truly desire. In times to comfort no less than in times of pain, we must always seek God. We must seek Him with diligence and determination, trusting that at the end our search He Himself, and He alone, will be our reward.

Two things are needed. We must *see* that our deepest need is for God, and we must then *seek* the fulfillment of that need in God only. The first of these is perhaps the hardest to do. On the surface, we seem to desire so many more visible and more immediate things that it's hard to understand how deeply we need God. But deeper than all our other wants is this ultimate desire: our longing for God. We long for Him because we were created for Him, and when we honestly and humbly recognize the importance of this need, we are then ready to seek God. We must devote ourselves wholeheartedly to finding Him, out most fervent hope being to come into His presence and enjoy His fellowship.

We tend not to seek God when our lives are comfortable. If our temporal needs are met, we imagine that we can take care of ourselves and we forget about God. For this reason, God lets us suffer some deprivation. The needs that go unmet may differ from person to person, but each of us will have our hearts broken in some ways. We will be taught to do without some of the things we deeply need, in order to learn that what we were created to enjoy is not fully available in this world. Only God can perfectly satisfy our hunger and our thirst, and He is always leading us in the direction of satisfaction in Him. He is teaching us, if we have the hearts to learn, that He is the only thing we can't do without.

Quote
> "All explorers are seeking something they have lost. It is seldom that they find it, and more seldom still that the attainment brings them greater happiness than the quest." --Arthur C. Clarke

Michael J Akers

4. The Will of God

What is God's will? Where do we begin to know His will? How does God guide you and me? How can God use you and me?

Following God's will means following God. Key Scriptures supporting this include:
- Numbers 22:1-38
- John 10:1-5, 27
- Luke 11:9-13
- John 7:16-19
- Heb 13:20-21
- Matt 7:21-23
- I Peter 3:13-18a
- Mark 1:16-20

Following God means to obey what is taught in Ephesians 4:25 though 5:21.

Read John 10:1-5 and 27, discuss the following questions:
- How are we similar and different to the sheep Jesus describes?
- What are the responsibilities of the sheep? of the shepherd?
- To what extent can we know where our shepherd is leading us?
- What things keep us from hearing Jesus as well as we could?
- What is one thing Jesus may be calling you to do today or this week?

Three ways to think about the will of God (1)
1. **Intentional will**—God's ideal plan for mankind. It was not the intentional will of God that Jesus should be crucified. His intention was that men would follow Jesus. It is never God's intentional will that humans should suffer. It is His intentional will that humans would have an abundant life, filled with joy and good health.
2. **Circumstantial will**—God's will within certain circumstances. When the evil in men created circumstances that made it necessary for Jesus to die, those circumstances caused the cross to become the will of God. Because of man's free will, circumstances are created that disturb God's intention for us. Yet, circumstances create a will within the intentional will of God. The circumstantial will of God enables us to find peace and wisdom expressed sp that ultimately the original plan of God is eventually realized.
3. **Ultimate will**—Final realization of God's purpose. It is His ultimate will that even through the evil of men, He will achieve His ultimate will, the redemption of mankind. God's ultimate will is the goal that He reaches, not only in spite of all that men may do, but also using mankind's evil to further His own plan. The power of God means that He has the ability to achieve His purpose for mankind. Nothing can happen that will defeat Him ultimately. God is able to achieve His ultimate purpose through the cross in spite of and and through the evil circumstances created by mankind.

Does God have a blueprint for everyone's life? If so, how fully can someone know God's blueprint for his/her life? In what ways does God reveal His will to us? How can we tell the difference between God's leading and our own inclinations? (2)
- The greatest means of discerning God's will is through deepening our friendship with Him. By this, we come to know and better understand what He wants. Friendship with Him results from time spent with Him (1) reading and knowing His Word (Psalm 40:8); (2) praying and meditating; (3) fellowship and counseling from other Christians; and (4) serving Him.
- We can also discern His will through (1) conscience; (2) common sense; (3) advice of friends through whom God uses; (4) great literature such as biographies of Christian leaders; (5) voice of the church;

(6) God speaking to our minds and hearts and we renew them (Rom 12:2)
- Clear evidence that you have found God's will is when you feel perfect peace in your life. It is the will of God that you have perfect peace (Psalm 40:8).

What situation in your life right now do you wish to know God's will?
- Do you really want to know His will or do you want Him to sanction your own will?
- Do you have the courage to do God's will when you discern it?

The Bible does indicate what is and what is not the will of God. Examples of what is not the will of God are
- Sexual immorality (I Thess 4:3)
- What is prohibited from the Ten Commandments
- What He hates in Proverbs 6:16-19

Examples of what is the will of God. These are not revealing His will for the future, but reveals His will for us everyday:
- Rejoice, pray, give thanks (I Thess 5:16-18)
- Submitting to Him and obeying Him (I Peter 2:13-15)
- Obeying parents (Eph 6:1)
- Marry a Christian (I Cor 6:15)
- Work (I Thess 4:11-12)
- Support family (I Tim 5:8)
- Give to God's work and to the poor (II Cor 8-9; Gal 2:10)
- Rear children to God's standards (Eph 6:4)
- Meditate on the Scriptures (Psalm 1:2)
- Assemble for worship (Heb 10:25)
- Proclaim Christ (Acts 1:8)
- Set proper values (Col 3:2)
- Spirit of gratitude (Phil 4:6)
- Display love (I Cor 13)
- Accept people without prejudice (James 2:1-10)
- Many more

Quotes
- "An individual's highest fulfillment, greatest happiness, and widest usefulness are to be found in living in harmony with the will of God" --John D. Rockefeller Jr.
- "I know God will not give me anything I cannot handle. I just wish He didn't trust me so much"-- Mother Teresa of Calcutta

5. The Grace and Mercy of God

What is the difference between grace and mercy?
- Grace is God giving to me what I do not deserve
- Mercy is God not doing to me what I deserve

Are gifts given by the grace of God unconditional?

Does salvation by grace through faith eliminate our need to meet conditions such as repentance, confession, and faithful living?

How do grace and mercy relate to works, law, and obedience?

<u>What does the Bible teach about grace?</u> (1)
- Grace is connected with two fundamental and eternal principles—
  o God must punish sin (Rom 6:23) because He inherently hates it. God cannot overlook sin. It is part of His divine nature that sin cannot be accepted; because God is God, sin must be punished.
  o All humans are sinners (Rom 3:23)
  o How can these two truths be reconciled? God's grace is the answer.
- Grace is NOT license nor is it legalism
  o License ignores the nature of God. We cannot ignore God's law and count on His grace to save us. License is perversion of God's grace. It denies the truth that God hates sin and always punishes it. Some think that Rom 5:19-21 teaches license, but Paul responds to this possibility in Rom 6:1,2,6,12. Grace is not the license to go on sinning! Peter also responds to the error of license in II Peter 3:11,14,17. Note how Peter concludes his admonishment in II Peter 3:18.
  o Legalism ignores the nature of humans to sin. Legalism believes that people will be saved by keeping the rules, that we have earned God's approval. The Bible is clear that no one can be saved by keeping the rules. Acts 15:10-11 argues against legalism; instead that salvation is because of God's grace. Paul said the same thing in Eph 2:8-9 and Gal 2:16.
- Grace IS God's work through Jesus (John 1:17).
  o Grace means that God became a man in the person of Jesus Christ. He became one of us. Jesus came for the purpose of keeping God's will perfectly in a human body -- that is why he was given a body in the first place. (Heb 10:5-7).
  o Grace means that Jesus took our place and paid the price for our sins (II Cor 5;19-6:1; I Peter 2:24).
  o Grace is received by true faith (Rom 5:1-2; Eph 2:8-9).
  o Personal question: Are you standing in God's grace?
  o Who specifically does God give grace to? (I Peter 5:5)

<u>What does the Bible teach about mercy?</u>
- God declared Himself to be a God of mercy (Exo 34:6)
- In Psalm 136, the refrain "His mercy (lovingkindness) endures forever" is repeated 26 times.
- God's mercy is what we appeal to when we ask for God's forgiveness (Ps 51:1)
- God says that He is pleased when we hope in His mercy (Ps 147:11)
- The greatest act of God's mercy—Jesus (Titus 3:5)
- God expects us to be merciful (Hosea 6:6; Micah 6:8; Matt 5:7, 23:23; Luke 6:36)
- God's wisdom is a wisdom that is full of mercy (James 3:17)

Questions

1. Why does there seem to be so little mercy?

2. What happens if we are not merciful? (James 2:13)

3. What blessings do God's grace and mercy offer you? Annette Vincelette, a mother of four who was one of the most dedicated followers of God on this earth, suffered for many years from a debilitating cancer of the spine that eventually killed her at age 54. During her suffering she said that Psalm 57 was a source of comfort and relief for her during her darkest hours.

Quotes

➢ "The greatest attribute of Heaven is mercy" --Francis Beaumont
➢ "Your worst days are never so bad that you are beyond the reach of God's grace; and your best days are never so good that you're beyond the need for God's grace" –unknown.

6. Creation

Days of Creation

Day 1	Genesis 1:3-5	Light (not the sun which was created on the fourth day)
Day 2	Genesis 1:6-8	Firmament (sky)-- the divider between the canopy of water in the sky from the water on the earth -Gen 2:5-6
Day 3	Genesis 1:9-13	Dry land (furnished with vegetation) separated from the water. Verse 9 indicates that there was a single land mass on earth surrounded by water.
Day 4	Genesis 1:14-19	Sun, moon and stars
Day 5	Genesis 1:20-23	Water creatures and fowl
Day 6	Genesis 1:24-31	Earth creatures and humans
Day 7	Genesis 2:2	Sabbath rest

Main Questions

1. Does Genesis have a gap of millions of years between Gen 1:1 and Gen 1:2?
2. Why not believe in evolution? (1)
   a. God is left out of creation—must reject Col 1:16; Psalm 24:11, 89:11, 139
   b. Dependency on chance
   c. Lack of evidence for species-to-species evolution
   d. Irreducible complexity of living things—too intricate as a whole to be evolved by steps
3. Can evolution be compatible with creation?
4. Actual length of days in Genesis?

There are 7 truths about creation that are foundations for our lives! (2)

1. God created everything out of nothing— Heb 11:3
2. Creation was done in proper order--(Gen 1:3-26). Can you recite the order of creation? Light—sky—water—land—plants/animals—mankind. God built order into astronomy, into biology, into ecology, into chemistry, into everything. How can anyone believe that order evolved out of chaos?
3. God saw that it was good. God richly gives us everything to enjoy— 1 Tim 6:17. Genesis records that after each day of creation God "saw that it was good". Some of the most destructive false teaching in the history of the church has revolved around the idea that creation is evil. Material things of this world are not inherently evil. It's what we do with God's creation that makes things evil. Money and sex are two great examples of this. We should enjoy what God has created, just don't turn it into something evil.
4. Man is the crown of creation--Gen 2:7 and 2:21-22. We were created from dust of the ground and from a rib. We are fingerprints of God; Steven Curtis Chapman wrote a song with this title. Is there not a more humbling truth in all of life that you and I were created in the image of God? What does that mean?
   a. Our personality: mind, will, emotions.
   b. Our sexuality: created as male and female. Both male and female have equal value and worth. Each race has equal value and worth.
   c. Our morality: created as moral beings, with a moral consciousness
   d. Our spirituality: created with the ability to relate to God
5. God finished the job.—Gen 2:1; Heb 4:3
6. God rested on the Seventh Day. By the seventh day God had finished the work he had been doing; so on the seventh day he rested from all his work. And God blessed the seventh day and made it holy, because on it he rested from all the work of creating that he had done.— Gen 2:2–3. Why did God rest? To give us an example to follow and to teach us his plan for the ages. If we don't rest,

that is rest that focuses on God, you'll eventually break down. How to rest is up to each person; don't let others tell you how to rest. To rest also means that spiritually we must enter into a trusting relationship with God and not always trust in our own works. Heb 4:9-11.

7. God now sustains all that He made—Col 1:17. These next few days, look to God who sustains the universe to give you sustaining strength throughout each day.

Four suggestions for how to praise God as our Creator God

1. Seeing creation as an expression of God's love.   Psalm 136:7-9, 25
2. Kneeling before God in humility.   Psalm 95:6-7
3. Praising God for each day.   Psalm 118:24
4. Thanking God for creating you.   Psalm 139:14

Questions

1. In what ways do you feel that your view of God as our Creator is impacting your daily thoughts about yourself and this world?
2. What is it that amazes you — simply amazes you — about the creation of God?
3. In what ways does God's creation speak to you specifically about the person and character of God? Example: when I look at the stars … at the ocean … at the Grand Canyon, etc.
4. Study and meditate on the following Scriptures: Psalm 104:31; Col 1:16; Psalm 24:1; Psalm 19:1-2; Gen 2:7; Gen 2:21-22.
5. What questions do you still have about creation vs. evolution? What can you NOT believe about the Biblical claims that God created everything from nothing? What main argument would you use against someone who does not believe in creation?

Quote

➢ "Any error about creation also leads to an error about God."—Thomas Aquinas

7. Faith and Faithfulness

What is the Biblical definition of faith? Heb 11:1, 6

What is the difference between faith and faithfulness? (1)
The author of Proverbs once sighed, "Many a man claims to have unfailing love, but a faithful man who can find?" (Prov. 20:6). The Psalmist also complained, "Help, LORD, for the godly are no more; the faithful have vanished from among men" (Psa. 12:1). We might well utter the same sigh and voice the same complaint today. We wonder, where are the truly faithful people? While most of us are quite familiar with faith, we may not be so familiar with the idea of faithfulness. The two concepts are closely related, but slightly different. Both faith and faithfulness spring from the same Hebrew root, *aman*. It is the same root from which we get our word "amen." Even the word "amen" expresses the idea of God's faithfulness, since it means, "verily," "it is steadfast," or "so be it."

God Is Faithful (2)
God is a God of faithfulness. He is a God of absolute reliability, of steadfast love, and of loyalty. He does not change his mind (Num. 23:19). He is a God who keeps his word forever (Isa. 40:8). He also keeps his promises and his covenants with man (Lam 3:23). Early in the Bible God reveals himself as the faithful God. God speaks through Moses in Deut 7:9 *"Know therefore that the LORD your God is God; he is the faithful God, keeping his covenant of love to a thousand generations of those who love him and keep his commands."* In Deut 32:4, God is said to be *"A faithful God who does no wrong".* All his works and his commandments reveal his faithfulness (Psalm 33:4, 46:1-4, 119:86).

It is clear in the Bible that God's faithfulness does not wear out with time. In Ps 119:90, the Psalmist declares of God, *"Your faithfulness continues through all generations...."*. God's faithfulness is particularly displayed in his eternal covenant love expressed to Israel (Hos 2:19-20). In the New Testament we continue to see an expression of the idea of God's faithfulness. In regard to Israel, Paul queries in Romans 11:1: *"I ask then: Did God reject his people...?* The apostle seems to be aghast at such an idea and exclaims *"...By no means!...."* (v.1). Even in regard to man and his feeble attempts at faithfulness, the apostle says, *"If we are faithless, he will remain faithful, for he cannot disown himself"* (2 Tim. 2:13).

The Bible teaches that Christ is faithful. In fact, in Rev 19:11, he is given the title of "Faithful and True." We learn that God is faithful and just to forgive our sins when we confess them to him (I John 1:9). He is faithful to help us (1 Cor. 1:9). He is loyal in regard to all he has promised us (Heb. 11:11). He is faithful to us, in that he will not allow our temptations to go beyond what we can endure (1 Cor. 10:13). God even promises to faithfully preserve his people until the second coming of Christ (1 Thess. 5:23; Phil 1:6).

God Expects Us To Be Faithful (2)
Since God is a faithful God and we are his children, we are expected also to be faithful. This quality is literally the hallmark of the Christian life. We see it mentioned as a characteristic of several early Christians ministers. For instance, there is Onesimus (Col. 4:9), Timothy (1 Cor. 4:17), and Epaphras (Col. 1:7). Our faithfulness is merely the necessary and expected response to God's faithfulness. Thus, faithfulness is something that is primarily expressed toward God. It simply means "full of faith" or "trustful."

However, faithfulness, if it is genuine, will also find expression in our relationships with others. It will affect the way we speak (Prov. 12:22). It will keep us from speaking about the secrets others have entrusted to us (Prov. 11:13). The expression of faithfulness in our lives will cause us to be esteemed by others who trust in us (Prov 25:13).

Jesus gives us several illustrations concerning the effects of faithfulness in the area of human dealings. In Luke 12:42 we see that a faithful and wise servant does what he has been instructed to do. We learn in Luke 16:10; *"He who is faithful in what is least is faithful also in much; and he who is unjust in what is least is unjust also in much"* The Apostle Paul goes on to tell us that it is required in stewards that a man be found faithful (1 Cor.4:2). We see reflected even in the New Testament the great emphasis upon deeds which has characterized Hebrew thought. In contrast, we Christians have often focused more upon creeds or proper theological definitions.

Faithfulness is said to be a fruit of the Spirit (Gal. 5:22), yet for so many supposedly Spirit-filled and Spirit-led people, there is less and less evidence of faithfulness. One example that comes up often today is the matter of keeping one's word and not being fickle. What a poor witness to our world when we cannot stand by our word and do what we have committed ourselves to do. God does not lead people to break their word or their vows. He expects us to follow his example, and keep our word. The Bible instructs us to keep our word, even when it works to our disadvantage. In Psalm 15:4, the writer speaks of the righteous man *"...who keeps his oath even when it hurts.... "*

There is another area of great unfaithfulness today in Christianity. It is the matter of our sacred agreements and life-long covenants with our wives and husbands. Just as God is faithful in his marriage relationship with Israel, and just as Christ is faithful in his marriage relationship with the church (Eph. 5:25), Christians are likewise to be faithful in their marriage relationships. This too is a sacred covenant relationship made before God, as we see in Malachi 2:14. Today the divorce rate among Christians has climbed slightly higher than the rate among non-Christians.

We need to make a lot of changes if we are to be faithful people. The scripture assures us that God will preserve the faithful man or woman (Psalm 31:23). In Psalm 101.6 we have this precious verse where God himself says: *"My eyes will be on the faithful in the land, that they may dwell with me; he whose walk is blameless will minister to me."*

Questions
1. Who exemplifies faith and faithfulness to you?
2. How do we obtain faith and then keep growing in our faithfulness? (Rom 10:13,14,17)
3. What did Jesus ask us to believe? (John 14:1, 7:38; 5:24; 3:14-18)
4. What are the benefits of faith? (Mark 9:23, John 1:12, John 3:16, 18; John 5:24, John 12:46, John 20:31)
5. What are barriers that keep us from being more faithful?
6. Discuss: Mark 9:24: *"I believe, help me in my unbelief"*

Quotes
➢ "I do not pray for success, I ask for faithfulness." Mother Teresa
➢ A little faith will bring your soul to heaven; a great faith will bring heaven to your soul. --Charles Spurgeon

8. Scripture and Truth

Studying Your Bible

How to study? Read ---> Interpret ---> Meditate ---> Memorize ---> Apply ---> Teach (Ezra 7:10)
"Reading gives breadth, Study gives depth". Study involves use of a pen.

Some basic questions:
1. How much time do you spend a day reading/studying your Bible?
2. Do you use a plan in your Bible reading and study?
3. Do you meditate on what you have read?

The Claims of the Bible (1)

1. The Bible is the source of TRUTH.
- Jesus said in John 17:17b "Thy Word is truth".
- Jesus said that He is the truth (John 14:6)
- Pilate asked "What is truth" (John 18:38a). Why was no answer recorded?
- Think of the millions of books published. Are any other available which ever present the complete truth of life that you can trust with your own life?
- Jesus said, "If you continue in My word....you shall know the truth and the truth shall make you free" (John 8:31b-32). What is the meaning of "free"?
- The Bible is <u>infallible</u>. It has no mistakes. (Psalm 19:7; 119:142,151,160). The Bible was authored by God and God is flawless. Everything it says is true.

2. The Bible is the source of HAPPINESS.
- "The statutes of the Lord are right, rejoicing the heart" (Psalm 19:8). As you study the Bible and learn its great truths, don't you get excited about what God does and can do in your life?
- Jesus said, "Blessed are those hear the word of God, and observe it". (Luke 11:28) What are the two requirements for being happy? Also read John 15:11; 16:33.
- Can anyone possibly read and meditate on Psalm 34:17-19 and not feel blessed (happy)? Are there other examples of you being uplifted after reading the Bible?
- Do you or have you ever experienced the sensation the disciples described in Luke 24:32 during or after you have spent quality time in the Scriptures?

3. The Bible is the source of VICTORY.
- We all like to win. When we lose, we don't like it. A Christian should strive for excellence, never giving the devil an occasion to take advantage of you (II Cor. 2:11).
- As we study the Bible, God's Word becomes a source of victory. Psalm 119:11 says that the Bible is the source of victory over sin. As the Word sinks in our hearts it becomes the resource with which the Holy Spirit uses to direct us. Without God's Word entering our conscious mind there is no way we can prevent sin from leading us!
- The Bible gives us victory over demons (Luke 4:33-36). One word spoken and Jesus showed His authority over a legion of demons.
- The Bible give us victory over temptation (Eph 6:17). Having the sword of the Spirit is not owning a Bible, but knowing the specific principles in the Bible that apply to the specific temptation.
- Here is a brief schematic to remember when fighting trials and temptations in our lives:

Source	Site of Attack	Time of Life	Solution	Scripture
Flesh	Body	Early Age	Flee	I Cor 6:18
World	Soul	Middle Age	Faith	I John 5:4-5
Devil	Spirit	Old Age	Fight	James 4:7

- There are many areas of temptation in our lives (e.g. sexual, greed, pride, drunkenness, lying, gossip, envy, vengeance, backsliding, dishonesty). In your specific temptation are you aware of what specific Scripture you can use to help to fight that temptation when it strikes?

- The Bible gives us victory over Satan (Matt 4:1-11). Satan tempted Jesus three times; yet each time Jesus quoted Scripture to defeat Satan. Capturing Biblical truth in our minds (Rom 12:2) gives us the capacity to defeat Satan and his attacks on us. We cannot do it on our own. Yet we still believe that we can be good, avoid temptation, and cannot commit sin using our own logic and resources. Do not be deceived! (Gal 6:7).
- The Bible assures us of our salvation and answered prayer (I John 5:13-14; John 15:7).
- The 5 "Ps" that describe a Christian--Pardon, Peace, Power, Provision, Purpose

4. The Bible is the source of GROWTH.

- One of the saddest things to see is the Christian who does not grow spiritually? Why? What does it mean to grow spiritually?
- There are five main reasons why Christians fail to grow spiritually--lack of understanding, lack of humility, lack of faith, lack of commitment, and lack of power. What is the one source that can counterattack each and all of these lackings (II Tim 3:16-17)?
- Going to church regularly, even attending a Bible class regularly does not mean spiritual growth automatically occurs.
- I Peter 2:2 says that growth is directly proportional to the amount of time and effort one spends in studying the Word of God. This is also referred to in Heb 5:13-14.
- A pre-requisite for growth is setting aside all evil things, confess our sin, get our life prioritized, and hit the Word with great desire--James 1:21, I Peter 2:1.
- Where are you right now in your spiritual growth? What is your plan to grow?

5. The Bible is the source of POWER.

- The more you know the Bible the more power you have because the less you will fear any situation. (Acts 1:8).
- How is the Bible a source of power? What do the following verses claim? Heb 4:12, Eph 4:23, Rom 1:16, Rom 12:2, II Cor 3:18.
- You can do everything you think. You can do above everything you can think. In fact, you can do exceedingly abundantly above and beyond all you can ask or think! (Eph 3:20)
- Isa 55:11 states that God's Word will accomplish what it says it will accomplish. The Word of God is not just words, but words backed by the power of the Holy Spirit (I Thess. 1:5). We are to have assurance that it will do exactly what it says it will do. Examples? Penalties of sin (Matt 18:6); Blessing of being humble and/or patient (James 1:2-4); Uplifting our spirit (Psalm 32:8, Psalm 34:17, Heb 13:5-6); Raising our children (Prov 22:6); Reaping what we sow (Gal 6:7); Using language (Prov 16:21, Eph 4:29); Comfort and strength during hard times (Psalm 37:4-5, Psalm 86, Gal. 6:9)

6. The Bible is the source of GUIDANCE.

- What is the will of God for your life? God tells you in His Word. Read Psalm 119:105. How did God lead all the different people in the Bible? Their situations may be similar to one with which you are struggling right now.
- The Holy Spirit in us is there to apply personally the Word that will give us the appropriate guidance for any situation that we are in (John 14:26, I John 2:27).
- Name an area of life where you feel you need guidance right now. The Bible has the answer!

Quote
- "It is not at all incredible, that a book which has been so long in the possession of mankind should contain many truths as yet undiscovered". -- Bishop Butler

9. God's Covenants

Covenant (Hebrew "berith": to eat with, to allot, mutual obligation). "A covenant is a sovereign pronouncement of God by which He establishes a relationship of responsibility (1) between himself and an individual, (2) between Himself and mankind in general, (3) between Himself and a nation, or (4) between Himself and a specific human family."

Three types of legal relationships in the Old Testament:
1. Two sided covenant between <u>human</u> parties, both of which voluntarily accept the terms of the agreement (e.g. friendship, marriage, political alliance). God never enters into such a convenant of equality with men.
2. One-sided disposition imposed by a superior party (e.g. Gen 2:17, Ezek 17:13-14, Josh 23:16, Hos 6:7)
3. God's self-imposed obligation for the reconciliation of sinners to Himself (Gen 17:7, Deut 7:6-8, Ps 89:3-4)

Covenants: Edenic, Adamic, Noachian, Abrahamic, Mosaic or Sinaitic, Levitical, Davidic, and New. (1,2)

The <u>Adamic Covenant</u> can be thought of in two parts: the <u>Edenic Covenant</u> (innocence) and the <u>Adamic Covenant</u> (grace) (Gen 3:16-19). The Edenic Covenant is found in Gen 1:26-30; 2:16-17. The Edenic Covenant outlined man's responsibility toward creation and God's directive regarding the tree of the knowledge of good and evil. The Adamic Covenant included the curses pronounced against mankind for the sin of Adam and Eve, as well as God's provision for that sin (Gen 3:15).

Noahic Covenant (Gen 6:18, 8:21-9:17) where God promises life and the preservation of the seed of the woman.

<u>Abrahamic Covenant</u> (Gen 12:1-3, 6-7; 13:14-17; 15; 17:1-14; 22:15-18). In this covenant, God promised many things to Abraham. He personally promised that he would make Abraham's name great (Gen 12:2), that he would have numerous physical descendents (Gen 13:16), and that he would be the father of a multitude of nations (Gen 17:4-5). God also made promises regarding a nation called Israel. In fact, the geographical boundaries of the Abrahamic covenant are laid out on more than one occasion in the book of Gen (12:7; 13:14-15; 15:18-21). Another provision in the Abrahamic covenant is that the families of the world will be blessed through the physical line of Abraham (Gen 12:3; 22:18). This is a reference to the Messiah, who would come from the line of Abraham.

<u>Mosaic Covenant</u> (Deut 11; II Cor 3:7-9; Rom 3:19-20; Heb 10:1-10). The Mosaic covenant was a conditional covenant that either brought God's direct blessing for obedience or God's direct cursing for disobedience upon the nation of Israel. Part of the Mosaic covenant was the ten commandments found in Exodus 20, but also the rest of the law which contained over 600 commands—roughly 300 positive and 300 negative. The history books of the Old Testament (Joshua-Esther) detail how Israel succeeded at obeying the law or how Israel failed miserably at obeying the law. Deut 11:26-28 details specifically the blessing/cursing motif.

<u>Palestinian Covenant</u> (Deut 30:1-10). The Palestinian covenant amplifies the land aspect which was detailed in the Abrahamic covenant. In this covenant, God, because of their disobedience, would cause the people of the nation to be scattered around the world (Deut 30:3-4), and that God would eventually restore the nation together (verse 5). When the nation is restored, then the nation will obey him perfectly (verse 8), and God will cause them to prosper (verse 9).

<u>Levitical Covenant</u> (Num 25:12-13) made reconciliation between God and man through priestly atonement

<u>Davidic Covenant</u> (II Sam 7:8-16). The Davidic covenant amplifies the seed aspect which was detailed in the Abrahamic covenant. The promises to David in this passage are very significant. God promised that David's physical line of descent would last forever and that his kingdom would never pass away permanently (verse 16). This kingdom, furthermore, would have a ruling individual exercising authority over it (verse 16). Obviously, the Davidic throne has not been in place at all times. There will be a time, however, when someone from the line of David will again sit on the throne and rule as king. This future king is Jesus (Luke 1:32-33).

<u>New Covenant</u> (Jer 31:31-34; Heb 8:7-13). The New covenant is a covenant made with the nation of Israel which speaks about the blessings which are detailed in the Abrahamic covenant. In the new covenant, God promises to forgive sin and there will be a universal knowledge of the Lord (v 34). It even appears that the nation of Israel will have a special relationship with their God (v 33). The New Covenant also can include Jesus' statements in Matt 26:26-28. Jesus instituted this covenant with his eleven disciples to become representatives of a new body of believers known as the church. They were called as Apostles to invite Jews and Gentiles alike around the world to enter into this New Covenant. After the completion of this calling out of the true church, Scripture promises that God will return and bring the nation of Israel (as a nation) into the New Covenant. This will take place at the end of the age when Jesus returns to Jerusalem to sit as King on the throne of His father David.

Under the new covenant all those (God's people) who belong to Christ and are part of the church benefit in the following ways (3):

Called children of God—Rom 8:16	Called "the Israel of God"---Gal 6:16
Called the household of God--Eph 2:19	Heirs of the kingdom---James 2:5
Called children of Abraham---Gal 3:7	Called " chosen generation…."I Peter 2:9
Called children of promise---Rom 9:8	Called "sons of God"---John 1:12
A "people of His own"---Titus 2:14	Kings and priests of God---Rev 1:6
Heirs of God according to promise---Gal 3:29	Called "Mount Zion", "The City of the Living God"---Heb 12:22
Called the temple of God---1 Cor 3:16	The Bride of Christ---2 Cor 11:2
Called "the circumcision"---Phil 3:3	The Body of Christ---1 Cor 12

<u>Questions:</u>
1. What is the practical meaning of covenant to us today?
2. Discuss what is meant by "He will make them know His covenant" (Psalm 25:14)
3. What does Jeremiah 31:31-34 really mean?
4. Since there are different covenants, does this mean that God has different plans for different people, i.e. Israel vs the Church?

<u>Quote</u>
➢ "Marriage has a unique place because it speaks of an absolute faithfulness, a covenant between radically different persons, male and female; and so it echoes the absolute covenant of God with His chosen, a covenant between radically different partners".**--Rowan D. Williams**

10. Fear/Reverence of God

<u>We are commanded to fear the Lord, to fear God.</u>
- "The fear of the Lord is the beginning of knowledge" (Prov 1:7)
- "The fear of the Lord is the beginning of wisdom" (Prov 9:10)
- "The conclusion, when all has been heard, is "fear God" and "keep His commandments" (Eccl 12:13)
- "Let all the earth fear the Lord; let all the inhabitants of the world stand in awe of Him". (Psalm 33:8)
- "The fear of the Lord leads to life" (Prov 19:23)
- "And do not fear those who kill the body, but are unable to kill the soul; but rather fear Him who is able to destroy both soul and body in hell" (Matt 10:28)

<u>We are to fear the Lord, but we are not to fear other people.</u>
- "The fear of man brings a snare" (Prov 29:25)
- "The Lord is for me, I will not fear, what can man do to me?" (Psalm 118:6)
- "Do not fear men….." (Matt 10:26, 28)

<u>What does it mean to "fear the Lord"? (1)</u>
The Hebrew word used in the Proverbs verses has the meaning of 'reverencing the Lord'. Reverence is to be in a state of humility toward God because we acknowledge His great power and authority. "The fear of the Lord" also means to hate evil, pride, arrogance, the evil way and a perverse mouth. If we have the "fear of the Lord" we will not only hate these things, we will resist them, and ask the Lord to deliver us from being guilty of these sins. When we tolerate evil in our lives and speak evil things, we are declaring that we have no fear of God. In fact, we have fallen into the sin of pride and arrogance, because we think that God is simply overlooking our sin and our wrong attitudes, just because we may appear to get by with some things at the present. God is a merciful God and He gives all of us time to repent, so that our own sins do not produce the effects of the sowing and reaping process.

In the New Testament, we read that "perfect love casts out fear." (1 John 4:18). What does this mean? This means that if we really love God we will not disobey Him. Therefore, if we do not disobey the Word of God, we have nothing to fear. We would not want to do anything that God does not want us to do, if we love God and desire to please Him. This does not mean that we have to be perfect, as we all fail God at times. It does mean that, because of our love for God, we will strive to obey Him perfectly.

Without the true fear of God, one is left knowing nothing (as in 1 Timothy 6:4), because the fear of the Lord is the *beginning* of knowledge (Prov 1:7). A person does not even begin to have knowledge if they do not fear God, as it is written, "fools hate knowledge" (Prov 1:22). Without the true fear of God, a person is a fool, because the true fear of God is also the *beginning* of wisdom (Ps 111:10). A person does not even begin to have wisdom if they do not fear God, as it is written, "fools despise wisdom and instruction" (Prov 1:7). The sad reality of all of this is the miserable state of mankind. There is no fear of God before their eyes. (Rom 3:18). They are fools (Ps 14:104).

<u>So why do we need to fear God? (2)</u>
- Anyone who knows God, knows fear means fear (i.e. to be afraid), especially when it comes to the Almighty. Because, both in His severity (Ps 90:11) and in His goodness (Jer 33:9; Luke 5:26; 7:16), He is terrifying.
- He is unique, and who can make Him change? And whatever His soul desires, that He does. "For He performs what is appointed for me, and many such things are with Him. Therefore I am terrified at His presence; when I consider this, I am afraid of Him. For God made my heart weak, and the Almighty terrifies me." (Job 23:13-16)

- God has the power, right, and will (according to what He sees fit, Ps 115:3) to destroy your life (as in Job 1 & 2) or bless it (as in Job 42:10; James 5:11), to save you from eternal torment (Heb 7:25), or to burn you in hell forever (e.g. Jude 7).
- He creates vessels of mercy and vessels of wrath (Rom 9:21-23) and destines people to either eternal life or eternal torment completely apart from anything they may or may not do (Rom 9:11), but solely based upon His will (Rom 9:16, 18) and His pleasure (Psalm 115:3; Eph 1:5).
- <u>Mercy</u> is only found within the power and will of the Almighty (Dan 9:9).
- Our God is the God of salvation, and to God the Lord belong escapes from death. (Ps 68:20)
- "Therefore men fear Him" (Job 37:24), because they know therein lies their only hope (Acts 4:12). For the Lord takes pleasure in those who fear Him, in those who hope in His mercy. (Ps 147:11; see also Luke 1:50; Acts 10:35)
- Serve the Lord with fear, and rejoice with trembling. (Psalm 2:11) In the true fear of God, fear and trembling and rejoicing in the Lord (Philippians 4:4) are harmonious as well.
- He who walks in his uprightness fears the Lord, but he who is perverse in his ways despises Him. (Prov 14:2). There is no way someone who fears God can continue in sin unrepentantly because by the fear of the Lord one *departs* from evil. (Prov 16:6). Those who fear God repent, and they love correction (Proverbs 12:1; 15:5); because they know it is the way of life (Prov 6:23).
- The fear of the Lord is to hate evil (Prov 8:13). Wisdom continues in Prov 8:13 stating that she hates pride, arrogance, the evil way, and the perverse mouth.
- In the fear of the Lord there is strong confidence, and His children will have a place of refuge. (Prov 14:26; Psalm 112:7-8)
- The true fear of God does not produce cowardice, but rather boldness, as Prov 28:1 says, The wicked flee when no one pursues, but the righteous are bold as a lion. Cowards go to hell (Rev 21:8), but the righteous, i.e. those who fear God, are in no way cowards, but are rather bold as a lion. God fearing people are able to live out serious confidence even in the face of horrifying circumstances.
- Whenever I am afraid, I will trust in You. In God (I will praise His word), in God I have put my trust; I will not fear. What can flesh do to me? (Psalm 56:3-4) The answer? Nothing. Nothing that God Himself has not already decreed (Isaiah 46:10).
- Since the fear of God is wisdom (Job 28:28), it is no wonder that those who fear God are taught by God, and therefore have the wisdom of God. Psalm 25:12 says, *Who is the man that fears the Lord? Him shall He teach in the way He chooses.* Those who fear God have an anointing from the Lord (I John 2:27) and receive special instruction from Him. As it is written: The secret of the Lord is with those who fear Him, and He will show them His covenant. (Psalm 25:12-14).

Questions
1. After studying this lesson and these verses, how would you define/describe "the fear of the Lord" to someone who might be intimidated by this phrase?
2. What has been a new learning for you about fearing the Lord?

Quote
➢ "Where there is fear of God to keep the house, the enemy can find no way to enter." - Francis of Assisi

11. Hope and Security

Billy Graham once said that being a Christian has three undeniable benefits: certainty, security, and peace of mind. Hope undergirds all three.

Biblical Definition of Hope
God inspired many of the OT and NT writers to write about hope. Hope is first mentioned in the Bible in Ruth 1:12. Hope was certainly part of mankind's psyche from the days of Adam and Eve after their sin, Noah surviving the flood, Abraham hoping God was faithful in His promises, and so forth. In the Old Testament, hope is mentioned most in the poetic books--Job, Psalms (esp 23, 37, 62), and Proverbs (esp 13). The prophet Jeremiah, both in the book named after him and the other book he wrote, Lamentations, uses the word "hope" several times, especially in Lamentations 3 (18, 21, 24, 26, 29).

There are many different Hebrew words for hope
- Tiqvah = cord = expectation (Psalm 71:5)
- Yachal = wait = (Lam 3:21)
- Miqveh = collection = something waited for = (Ezra 10:2)

The Greek word for hope is "elpizo" or "elpis" = to expect, to have confidence, to anticipate with pleasure. Interestingly, Jesus used this word only once and that was in Luke 6:34 in the context of a lender of money expecting or hoping to receive repayment. Titus 2:13 refers to Jesus as the "blessed hope"

The rest of the NT has a lot to say about hope with some of the more familiar passages being
- Romans 5:3-5; 8:24; 15:4
- I Cor 13:13
- Col 1:27
- I Tim 1; 4:10
- I Peter—see below
- Heb 6:19; 11:1

I Peter—The Book of Hope
The book called I Peter has been called the book of hope. Peter 1:3-9 gives us four truths about hope (1):

The origin and foundation of genuine hope (v 3) God is the origin and Jesus is the foundation of our genuine hope. Jesus is our LIVING HOPE. If God brought Jesus through the most painful trials and back from the dead, certainly He can bring us through whatever we face in this world, no matter how deep or serious our problems are. To those who do not have a personal relationship with Christ, hope is nothing more than fantasyland. We are promised that what we are dealing with now is not the end of the story.

The durability of genuine hope (v 4) We are promised an inheritance in heaven that cannot be taken away from us, nothing can destroy or defile or diminish or displace what we have waiting for us. This hope lasts forever! Definition of eternity!

The power of genuine hope (v 5): Think of the power of a raging sea, a severe thunderstorm, an earthquake, or any other natural event that God created. The power of God is much more powerful. How powerful is the presence of hope in our lives. We are protected by God, we are divinely protected. When our hope runs low because of all the disorder and disease and pain that life offers, remember to accept the mystery of all this misfortune and suffering. We will never be able to explain it. Yet, we can make up our minds to trust God to protect us from ever giving up our hope by His power from now throughout eternity.

The wonder of genuine hope (v 8-9) "….though you do not see Him now, but believe in Him, you greatly rejoice with joy inexpressible……"). Isn't it a wonder that the faithful Christian loves a person we have never seen and long to go to a place we have never visited? Ever wonder why God guarantees deliverance of our souls into life eternal when we don't deserve this?

So, what is hope?
Hope to go on, though we're scattered aliens on this earth
Those who leave suicide notes usually have the word "hopeless" either written or inferred. Karl Menninger stated, "Hope is the major weapon against the suicide impulse." Life is not hopeless, not if you ask God to take over the bits and pieces of your fragmented life and put them back together again.

Hope to grow up, even though we have failed and fallen
Thoreau once said that 'the mass of men lead lives of quiet desperation'. You might feel that you have no hope because you have done something very wrong or you know that you have failed someone and have stumbled in many ways. Yet, the great wonder of hope in the Lord is the fact that He will take us where we are today and help us to grow into someone very different, someone who will do mighty things for the Lord. Faith in Jesus, during the good times and the bad, keeps us from fitting the description of Thoreau. Our future is never hopeless if we seek the Lord.

Hope to endure, even though life hurts
Do you do what I do…..wake up in the morning all hopeful that your day will be filled with good and great things, that you will be encouraged and appreciated and recognized and fulfilled……but as the day progresses you find that all that you hoped for didn't happen? Thornton Wilder once said that hope is a projection of the imagination….so also is despair. Despair all too readily embraces the ills it foresees; hope is an energy that arouses the mind to explore every possibility to combat these ills. Hope is an energy that if we let Him, God will be there when we turn to Him, and enable us never to give up our hope.

Hope to believe, even though dreams fade
A person can go on without wealth and even without purpose for a while. But he will not go on without hope. In fact, take away our hope and we are plunged into the deepest darkness. Hope is when we believe God will say to us in our darkest hours, "That's far enough". Like Spring that follows winter, hope in God coming through for us revives and washes us and enables us to blossom again. In the movie, Shawshank Redemption, this statement is made a couple of times, "Hope is a good thing, maybe the best thing".

Questions
1. How are faith and hope similar, yet different?
2. Claim one or more of the above Scriptures (or one not listed) and write your greatest hope right now.

Quotes
➢ "He who has health, has hope. And he who has hope, has everything."—Old Proverb
➢ "Everything that is done in the world is done by hope."-- Martin Luther King, Jr.
➢ "What oxygen is to the lungs, such is hope to the meaning of life."—Emil Brunner.

12. God's Protection and Guidance

We often pray for God's protection and guidance, but what are we really praying for? What are we asking for protection from and for guidance to?

Protection (1)

Verse	What the Verse says about God's Protection
Joshua 1:5	God's protection never leaves.
II Samuel 22	David's Psalm of praise because of God's protection
Psalm 5	Prayer for God's protection from the wicked
Psalm 18:2	God is our protector.
Psalm 56:9	God protects us from our enemies.
Psalm 57:1	God protects us until disaster has passed.
Psalm 91:3-7	God protects us from danger.
Psalm 121:3-8	God is always protecting us.
Psalm 124:1-5	God's protection is necessary.
Isaiah 41:10	God's protection is reassuring.
1 Corinthians 10:13	God protects us while we are being tempted.
John 10:28-30	God's protection is powerful.
2 Thessalonians 3:3	God protects us from evil.
2 Timothy 4:17-18	God strengthens us and rescues us.

Questions on Protection
1. What forces or circumstances in life do Christians most need God's protection?

2. What force(s) or circumstance(s) are in your life where you need God's protection?

3. What one verse above (or another verse you claim) speaks most clearly to you?

4. Describe a situation in your life when you felt God's protection

Prayer of Protection
The first U.S. astronauts to the moon took the following poem with them: Say this prayer from your heart, it works!

> The light of God surrounds me;
> The love of God enfolds me;
> The power of God protects me;
> The presence of God watches over me;
> Where ever I am God is.
> --James Dillet Freeman

Guidance
God has a definite and set plan for your life - and He will now be the One to guide you every step of the way into the fulfillment of that plan!   And not only does God have a set plan and a set future for your life - but He also has a set timetable in which all of these plans will manifest in your life. You simply have to learn to have patience during these waiting periods. This is where you have to learn how to have **complete faith in the Lord** to do all of this for you.

Guidance

Verse	What the Verse says about God's Guidance
Psalm 32:8	"I will instruct you and teach you in the way should go; I will guide you with My eye upon you"
Psalm 37:4,7, 23	"Delight yourself also in the Lord, and He shall give you the desires of your heart. Commit your way to the Lord, trust also in Him, and He shall bring it to pass ... Rest in the Lord, and wait patiently for Him. The steps of a good man are ordered by the Lord ... "
Psalm 48:14	"For this is God, our God forever and ever; He will be our guide even to death."
Proverbs 1:33	"But whoever listens to me will dwell safely, and will be secure, without fear of evil."
Proverbs 3:5-6	"Trust in the Lord with all your heart, and lean not on your own understanding; in all your ways acknowledge Him, and He shall direct your paths."
Proverbs 16:9	"A man's heart plans his way, but the Lord directs his steps."
Isaiah 48:17	Thus says the Lord, Your Redeemer, the Holy One of Israel: "I am the Lord your God, who teaches you to profit, who leads you by the way you should go."
Isaiah 58:11	"The Lord will guide you continually ..."
Jer 10:23	"O Lord, I know the way of man is not in himself; it is not in man who walks to direct his own steps."
Jer 29:11	"For I know the thoughts that I think toward you, says the Lord, thoughts of peace and not of evil, to give you a future and a hope."

Questions on Guidance
1. Discuss as specifically as possible the meaning of Proverbs 3:5-6.
2. What are examples in your life where you have been led by God to make the best decisions?

Quotes
➤ "God speaks to us through our desires, then as we lay them at His feet, He helps us sort them out and quiets our hearts to accept what He has already prepared." Rosalind Rinker
➤ "God often takes a course for accomplishing His purposes directly contrary to what our narrow views would prescribe. He brings a death upon our feelings, wishes, and prospects when He is about to give us the desire of our hearts." John Newton

13. Heaven, Hell, and Eternity

Hell (1)
God will send people to hell who are judged to be absent of personal righteousness (John 3:36, Matt 25:31-46, Matt 8:12) that only comes through believing in Jesus Christ. Today, when the wicked die, they go to a place called Hades where they await final judgment (Luke 16:20-25, Rev 20:11-15).

Hell is a place of
- everlasting punishment (Matt 25:46)
- everlasting fire (Matt 18:8)
- everlasting chains (II Thess 1:8)
- the eternal fire (Jude 7)
- the pit of the abyss (Rev 9:2,11)
- outer darkness (Matt 8:12)
- the wrath of God (Rom 2:5)
- eternal destruction (II Thess 1:9)
- eternal sin (Mark 3:29)
- torment (Mark 9:43-4

Three words in the New Testament describe hell
> *Tartarus* (II Peter 2:4, Jude 6)
> *Gehenna* (13 times; 12 by Christ, e.g. Mark 9:44,46,48; once in James 3:6)
> *Hades* (Luke 16:23)

Gehenna was a real place, a garbage dump in a valley outside Jerusalem, a place where the city garbage and bodies of executed criminals were dumped, where worms and fire existed. Also referenced in Josh 15:8, II Kings 23:10, and Neh 11:30).

Heaven
Those saved in Christ go to a place called Paradise (Luke 23:42-43) where their souls will reside until the Second Coming of Christ; at which time a new heaven and a new earth will be established (II Peter 3:10-13, Rev 21:1-7) and we will receive eternal bodies (I Cor 15:42-44).

Heaven is described primarily in Rev 21. Other descriptions are found in Rev 7:15-17, Rev 22:1-6, and other singular verses of Scripture. What will heaven be like?
- Brand new (Rev 21:1, 5; Isa 65:17)
- No sea = chaos, danger (Rev 21:1)
- God will dwell directly with us (Rev 21:3)
- No more mourning, crying, pain, or death (Rev 21:4)
- Complete, whole love, no more prioritization (no marriage) (Matt 22:23-30)
- We will fit, home will be perfect, it's where we belong (Phil 3:20, John 14:2-3)
- We will have crowns, but not wear them (Rev 4:10)
  - o Crown of life (James 1:12)
  - o Crown incorruptible (I Cor 9:24-27)
  - o Crown of rejoicing (I Thess2:19-20)
  - o Crown of righteousness (II Tim 4:5-8)
  - o Crown of glory (I Peter 5:2-4)
  - o Rewards of the believer's works (Luke 12:33, I Cor 3:11-15, II Cor 5:10)
- We will have complete knowledge and understanding of all things (I Cor 13:12)
- Everything is reconciled (Rev 22:2)

- Work continues (Rev 7:15-17)
- No more sun or moon (Rev 7:16, 21:23, 22:5)
- No more hunger, thirst, or heat (Rev 7:16)

God is not as concerned about getting you to heaven as He is about getting heaven into you!

Eternity

We humans really cannot understand eternity. How can anyone truly define something that is infinite?[1] We also cannot really define "God" because God is eternal. Eternity is not mentioned much in Scripture (Eccl 3:11, Micah 5:2, Rom 1:20, I Tim 1:17); however, eternal life is mentioned many times, all in the New Testament.

Eternal life (Greek "aiónios zoé") means infinity of time. Eternal life for the Christian has its beginning in the mind of eternal God (Eph 1:4) and our experience of it begins with the new birth in Christ (John 3; Titus 3:4-7). Eternal life is most prominent in the gospel of John and in I John, but also is mentioned in the other gospels, Acts, and the epistles of Romans Galatians, I Timothy, Titus, and Jude.

Read and discuss what is taught about eternity and eternal life in the following verses:
- John 3:15-16, 36
- Matt 19:16-29 (also Mark 10:17-22 and Luke 10:25-37; 18:18-27)
- John 6:27, 40, 47, 54, and 68
- John 11:25-26
- I Tim 6:12
- I John 1:1-4

Questions

1. What happens after death?
2. Will we be able to see and know our friends and family members in Heaven?
3. How can I know for sure that I will go to Heaven when I die?
4. Can people in heaven look down and see those of us who are still on the earth?
5. Why are people seemingly not afraid of eternal hell?
6. Are there different levels of punishment in hell?
7. What is paradise? Is it different than heaven? Where do people go when they die until Christ comes back?
8. What will we look like in Heaven?
9. What will we be doing in Heaven? Won't it get boring if we are there forever?
10. Will we remember our earthly lives when we are in Heaven?

Quote

➤ "I am not going to heaven because I've preached to great crowds of people. I'm going to heaven because Christ died on that cross. None of us is going to heaven because he's good. And we're not going to heaven because we've worked. We're not going to heaven because we pray and accept Christ. We're going to heaven because of what He did on the cross. All I have to do is receive Him. And it's so easy to receive Christ that millions stumble over its sheer simplicity."--Billy Graham

---

[1] There is a 1000 cubic foot rock on a remote island. Every 1000 years one bird lands upon that rock and sharpens its beak. When that rock has been completely eroded through infinitesimal beak sharpenings every 1000 years, a moment of eternity shall have passed.

Study Topics on God The Son

14. Sin

<u>What is sin? (1)</u>
Dr. Charles Ryrie has given a listing of Hebrew and Greek words that describe sin. In the <u>Hebrew</u> there are at least eight basic words:

- ra, bad (Gen 38:7)
- rasha, wickedness (Exo 2:13)
- asham, guilt (Hos 4:15)
- chata, sin (Exo 20:20)
- avon, iniquity (I Sam 3:13)
- shagag, err (Isa 28:7)
- taah, wander away (Ezek 48:11)
- pasha, rebel (I Kings 8:50).

The usage of these words leads to certain conclusions about the doctrine of sin in the O.T.
1. Sin was conceived of as being fundamentally disobedience to God.
2. While disobedience involved both positive and negative ideas, the emphasis was definitely on the positive commission of wrong and not the negative omission of good. In other words, sin was not simply missing the right mark, but hitting the wrong mark.
3. Sin may take many forms, and the Israelite was aware of the particular form which his sin did take.

The New Testament uses twelve basic <u>Greek</u> words to describe sin.

- kakos, bad (Rom 13:3)
- poneros, evil (Matt 5:45)
- asebes, godless (Rom 1:18)
- enochos, guilt (Matt 5:21)
- hamartia, sin (I Cor 6:18)
- adikia, unrighteousness (I Cor 6:9)
- anomos, lawlessness (I Tim 2:9)
- hupocrites, hypocrite (I Tim 4:2).
- parabates, transgression (Rom 5:14)
- agnoein, to be ignorant (Rom 1:13)
- planan, to go astray (I Cor 6:9)
- paraptomai, to fall away (Gal 6:1)

From the uses of these words several conclusions may also be drawn.
1. There is always a clear standard against which sin is committed.
2. Ultimately all sin is a positive rebellion against God and a transgression of His standards.
3. Evil may assume a variety of forms.
4. Man's responsibility is definite and clearly understood.

The word that is used most frequently is hamartia, missing the mark. It is the most comprehen-sive term for explaining sin. Paul used the verb hamartano when he wrote, "For all have sinned, and come short of the glory of God" (Rom 3:23). The flat statement of the Almighty is that all men have fallen far short of God's required standard. It is the popular and common practice of men to create their own standards; however, God has established His standard of perfection for entry into Heaven, and all men have "missed the mark" as an archer's bow would fall to the ground because it fell short of its target.

<u>From all of the above, sin exists in three basic forms</u>
1. <u>Disobedience of the law of God</u>. Jesus gave a very important/valuable lesson about the underlying

principle of sin. Read Matt 5:21,22,27,28. Jesus taught here that sin includes not only our physical actions, but also our thoughts and attitudes. Sin starts in the mind. When we allow evil thoughts to enter our mind and stay there, eventually these evil thoughts can spring into action, leading us to sin. We are what we think (Prov 23:7). Jesus told those of His day who were obsessed with physical cleanliness and ritual washings that it isn't what goes into our bodies that defile us, but the evil that is already there in our minds that debases us (Matt 15:17-20).

2. Sensuality. Read Luke 18:10-14, Gal 5:19-21. This kind of sin is what most people think of first. However, this kind of sin is not at the center of the Biblical doctrine of sin. The Pharisees did not commit this kind of sin, but Christ called them worse than prostitutes, drunks, or tax collectors. Again, it is not just the outward act itself that is sinful, it is what is within our hearts that is the real source of sin.

3. Pride. Pride is rebellion against God because we want to take God's place as judge of good vs evil. Pride was the main sin of Adam and Eve. It was their pride that gave them the desire to know good and evil. Pride at its worse is wanting to be good by ourselves without depending on God. The desire to be like God is enmity against our fellowman. Recall examples of evil leaders who thought they were like God. The desire to be like God cuts us off from God. Pride causes a human to become a slave to his own self-deception, arrogance, and inhumanity. Pride describes Satan.

Consequences of Sin
1. Total depravity—Romans 1:24-32; I Tim 4:2
2. Death—Roman 6:23; I John 3:14

Other Aspects of Sin
1. Rom 14:23—if we compromise our conscience we destroy our character
2. James 4:17—sins of omission. The four Gospels are filled with examples of this sin (e.g Matt 25:31-43, 46: Luke 12:16-21; Luke 16:19-31). Jesus often clashed with those who were diligent about strict literal obedience to God's laws but never realized God expects more of us. In Christ's day the Pharisees referred to detailed lists of what could and couldn't be done lawfully on the Sabbath; they were diligent about tithing down to the last seed or grain of spice; they spent hours studying the law, fasting and praying. Yet Christ called them "blind guides," "hypocrites" and a "brood of vipers."
3. Gal 5:16-- God's Spirit working within us will help us recognize sin and avoid it so we no longer will "fulfill the lust of the flesh." His Spirit will likewise help us recognize, understand and grow in His ways, enabling us to strengthen and demonstrate our faith through the works that James pointed out are necessary.
4. Psalm 38—what sin does to a person.
5. There are at least 667 sins listed in the Bible (2)

Quotes
➢ "Should we all confess our sins to one another we would all laugh at one another for our lack of originality"—Kihlil Gibran
➢ "The trouble with a little sin is that it doesn't stay little"—Unknown
➢ "He that has slight thoughts of sin never has great thoughts of God"—Owen
➢ "Sin has many tools, but a lie is the handle that fits them all."--Oliver Wendell Holmes
➢ "After the first blush of sin comes its indifference."--Henry David Thoreau
➢ "Our sense of sin is in proportion to our nearness to God"—Thomas Bernard

15. Jesus

What does "Jesus Christ" mean?
 Jesus (Iesous *ee-ay-sooce*) is Greek translation of Joshua, means "Savior".
 Christ ("Christos") means anointed, i.e. The Messiah = King

The most popular Bible verses (1) have been revealed after an internet survey of 37 million Bible references. All are about Jesus.
1. For God so loved the world, that he gave his one and only Son, that whoever believes in him should not perish, but have eternal life--John 3:16
2. In the beginning was the Word, and the Word was with God, and the Word was God--John 1:1
3. Jesus said to him, "I am the way, the truth, and the life. No one comes to the Father, except through me--John 14:6
4. Go , and make disciples of all nations, baptizing them in the name of the Father and of the Son and of the Holy Spirit--Matt 28:19
5. For all have sinned, and fall short of the glory of God--Romans 3:23

Why did Jesus come to earth?
1. To fulfill prophecy....examples:
   - His birthplace: Micah 5:2
   - Virgin birth: Isa 7:14
   - Time of His coming: Dan 9:24-26
   - Stem of Jesse: Isa 11:10
   - His Kingdom: Isa 9
   - To conquer death: Isa 25:8
   - To be our redeemer: Isa 59
   - His entrance into Jerusalem: Zech 9:9
2. Events of His suffering and death: Ps 41:9,   Isa 50:6; Ps 69:21; Ps 22:16; Ps 22:1
3. To reveal God to man—many examples: the Sermon on the Mount, Matt 16:16, John 14:28, I John 1:5, 2:17, 2:23, 3:3, 3:20, and see Jesus' key message below.
4. To offer His life as a sacrifice for the sins of men—I Peter 1:18-19, Eph 2:13, I Peter 3:18, Col 1:20, Rom 5:9, Rom 8:33-34, I John 1:7

Jesus' key messages included (2):
1. God loves you and is with you— John 14:23, John 14:21, John 3:16, John 15:9, John 10:27
2. Love one another -- Matt 7:12, 22:37-40; John 13:14-14, 13:34-35, Luke 6:35, Mark 10:43-45
3. Immense value of each person-- Matt 6:26, Matt 10:29-31, Matt 18:12, Luke 15:8-10
4. Good news: kingdom of God has come to earth--Luke 4:43, Mark 1:15, Matt 24:14, Matt 1:1, Matt 6:9-10, Luke 17:20-21, Luke 11:20, Luke 10:8-9, John 18:36
5. Reality of judgment to heaven or hell--Matt 12:36-37, Matt 13:41-43, Matt 18:23-35, Matt 25:31-46, Matt 7:21, Matt 10:32-33, Matt 18:3-4
6. God forgives those who ask--Matt 9:2, Luke 24:46-47, John 3:16-17, John 5:24, Matt 9:12-13, Luke 7:41, Luke 7:47, Matt 18:23-35.

Top Ten "Hardest To Understand" Statements That Jesus Said
   - "None of you can become my disciple if you do not give up all your possessions" (Luke 14:33).
   - "Whoever comes to me and does not hate father and mother, wife and children, brothers and sisters, yes, and even life itself, cannot be my disciple" (Luke 14:26).
   - "Do you think that I have come to bring peace to the earth? No, I tell you, but rather division! From now on five in one household will be divided........." (Luke 12:51-53)
   - "You have heard the law that says, 'Love your neighbor' and hate your enemy. But I say, love your enemies! Pray for those who persecute you! In that way, you will be acting as true children of your

Father in heaven (Matt 5:43-45).
- "You know that the rulers in this world lord it over their people, and officials flaunt their authority over those under them. But among you it will be different. Whoever wants to be a leader among you must be your servant, and whoever wants to be first among you must be the slave of everyone else. For even the Son of Man came not to be served but to serve others and to give his life as a ransom for many." (Mark 10:42-45)
- "If any of you wants to be my follower, you must turn from your selfish ways, take up your cross, and follow me. If you try to hang on to your life, you will lose it. But if you give up your life for my sake and for the sake of the Good News, you will save it. And what do you benefit if you gain the whole world but lose your own soul? (Mark 8:34-36)
- "And if your right eye makes you stumble, tear it out and throw it from you for it is better for you that one of the parts of your body perish than for your whole body to be thrown into hell (Matt 5:29; also 30)
- "Not everyone who says to Me, 'Lord, Lord' will enter the Kingdom of Heaven, but he who does the will of My Father, who is in heaven. Many will say to Me on that day, Lord did we not prophesy in Your name and in Your name cast out demons and in Your name perform many miracles? And I will declare to them "I never knew you, depart from Me, you who practice lawlessness" (Matt 7:21-23)
- "Blessed is he who keeps from stumbling over Me" (Matt 11:6)
- "And I say to you, that every careless word that men shall speak, they shall render account for it in the day of judgment" (Matt 12:36)

The Seven "I am" Statements That Jesus Claimed About Himself

"I Am" Statement	Verse	Description	Explanation
The bread of life	John 8:32	The Sustainer	He gives us all we need
The light of the world	John 8:12	The Illuminator	He brings the energy of light into our dark world
The door	John 10:9	The Mediator	He brings us where we otherwise could not go
The good shepherd	John 10:11	The Caretaker	He cares for us just like we need it
The resurrection and the life	John 11:25	The Life Giver	He brought us from death into life eternal
The way and the truth and the life	John 14:6	The Leader	He guides us through all of life's difficult ways
The true vine	John 15:1	The Success Maker	He makes us unbelievably productive

Questions
1. Who is Jesus Christ to you?
2. How does a person know Jesus Christ personally?
3. Study the following chapters and write down all the characteristics of the personality of Jesus and all the benefits He bestows upon us, His children: John 1, 10; 17; Phil 2: Col 3

Quotes
➤ "I like your Christ, I do not like your Christians. Your Christians are so unlike your Christ"—Gandhi
➤ "Jesus of Nazareth, without money and arms, conquered more millions than Alexander the Great, Caesar, Mohammed, and Napoleon; without science and learning, he shed more light on things human and divine than all philosophers and scholars combined; without the eloquence of school, he spoke such words of life as were never spoken before or since, and produced effects which lie beyond the reach of orator or poet; without writing a single line, he set more pens in motion, and furnished themes for more sermons, orations, discussions, learned volumes, works of art, and songs of praise than the whole army of great men of ancient and modern times." P. Schaff

16. The Cross

What comes to mind when you think of the cross?
- The actual physical structure
- Instrument of terrible torture and suffering
- Representative of the salvation of God through Jesus Christ
- Other thoughts/images/definitions?

What did God through Jesus accomplish with the cross?
1. Jesus Christ died on the Cross and poured out all His blood. He had to pour out His blood in order to pay for our sins, and to wash all our sins away.
2. The moment Jesus died on the cross, God, the Father, placed all those who would believe in Jesus, in advance, to die with Him on the Cross.
3. Jesus did not stay dead. Three days later He rose from the dead. He rose by the power of God, who was not willing to keep Him in the grave, because it was not for His own sins that He died, but for our own.
4. By believing that Jesus died for our sins and accepting His sacrificial death and resurrection, you are reborn and from that moment on the Lord is going to work by His Spirit to make manifest this resurrected Life in every area of your life. Jesus has already accomplished this for us in advance, because He is our life, and He lives in us.

The meaning of the cross (1)
Teaching on the cross is not a popular topic. Many people are offended or "grossed out" to think about the cross and what happened. The cross is hated by the world:
- "...the message of the cross is foolishness to those who are perishing, but to us who are saved it is the power of God." 1 Cor 1:18
- "For many walk, of whom I have told you often, and now tell you even weeping, that they are the enemies of the cross of Christ; whose end is destruction, whose god is their belly, and whose glory is in their shame -- who set their mind on earthly things....." Phil 3:18-19

Yet Paul emphasized that the cross is perhaps the most important foundational truth of the Christian faith;
- "For I determined not to know anything among you except Jesus Christ and Him crucified." (1 Cor 2:2)
- "But God forbid that I should boast except in the cross of our Lord Jesus Christ, by whom the world has been crucified to me, and I to the world" (Gal 6:14)
- "Knowing this, that our old man was crucified with Him, that the body of sin might be done away with, that we should no longer be slaves of sin." (Romans 6:4)
- "For Christ also suffered once for sins, the just for the unjust, that He might bring us to God, being put to death in the flesh but made alive by the Spirit." (1 Peter 3:18)

The meaning and the message of the cross is at the heart of all true gospel preaching.

Jesus was the Lamb of God, slain for our sins. John the Baptist, the greatest man of God until the time of Christ, cried out concerning Jesus, "Behold the Lamb of God, that takes away the sins of the world". Your sins and mine caused the innocent Son of God to be cruelly slain. What did Jesus ever do to deserve that? He was kind and gracious. He lived a pure life. He lived to bless others. He did good to people. Why did He die? On the cross He died for your sin, he died for my sin. Our sins put the nails into the Son of God. Our guilt was put upon Him. He did it, because of Love. A lot was achieved through the death of this Sacrificial Lamb on the cross. The greatest achieve-ment of all was the provision for our sins to be taken away. And not only our sins, but the sins of the whole world (1 John 2:2). Promises of the cross for Christians who believe that Jesus truly died on it for the forgiveness of our sins, for living our daily lives to glorify Him and for the hope of eternal live—Gal 2:20; Luke 24:6-8; Rom 6:3-7; II Cor 5:20-21; Eph 2:1-9; Col 1:20; 2:13-15.

Jesus' Seven Statements on the Cross

Statement	Verses	Main Teaching	Principle
Father, forgive them, for they know not what they do	Luke 23:34	Forgiveness	Main principles on forgiveness taught in Matt 18:21-35
Truly, I say to you, today you shall be with Me in Paradise	Luke 23:43	Salvation	Assurance of salvation (see I John 5:11-13). We need to share His plan of salvation with others
Woman, behold your son. Behold, your mother	John 19:26-27	Provision	We must provide for our loved ones (I Tim 5:8) and love them sacrificially (Eph 5, 6)
My God, My God, why hast Thou forsaken Me?	Matt 27:46 Mark 15:34	Questioning	We should not hesitate to pour out our hearts to God and ask for His help (Rom 8:18-28)
I am thirsty	John 19:26	Thirsting	Express to God how you thirst to know Him, how you thirst to have Him meet your deepest needs and the needs of your loved ones (Psalm 42:1-2, Heb 4:15-16)
It is finished	John 19:30	Purpose	Ask God to clarify His purpose for your life and to live your life in a focused way (Prov 16:3)
Father, into Thy Hands I commit My Spirit	Luke 23:46	Surrender	Surrender everything in your life and lifestyle to Him (Psalm 31, Col 3:17)

Discuss these verses that emphasize the cross and the Christian's responsibilities
- "He said to them all, 'If anyone desires to come after Me, let him deny himself, and take up his cross daily, and follow Me. Luke 9:23
- " And whoever does not bear his cross and come after Me cannot be My disciple. For which of you, intending to build a tower, does not sit down first and count the cost..." Luke 14:27-28
- "... he who does not take his cross and follow after Me is not worthy of Me. He who finds his life will lose it, and he who loses his life for My sake will find it." Matt 10:38-39
- "Then Jesus, looking at him, loved him, and said to him, 'One thing you lack: Go your way, sell whatever you have and give to the poor, and you will have treasure in heaven; and come, take up the cross, and follow Me.'" Mark 10:21
- "Christ did not send me to baptize, but to preach the gospel, not with wisdom of words, lest the cross of Christ should be made of no effect." 1 Cor 1:17
- "...if I still preach circumcision [conforming to accepted cultural standards], why do I still suffer persecution? Then the offense of the cross has ceased." Gal 5:11
- "...since we are surrounded by so great a cloud of witnesses, let us lay aside every weight, and the sin which so easily ensnares us, and let us run with endurance the race that is set before us, looking unto Jesus, the author and finisher of our faith, who for the joy that was set before Him endured the cross, despising the shame, and has sat down at the right hand of the throne of God." Heb 12:1-2

Quotes
➢ "All God's plans have the mark of the cross on them, and all His plans have death to self in them." --E. M Bounds
➢ "Men have said that the cross of Christ was not a heroic thing, but I want to tell you that the cross of Jesus Christ has put more heroism in the souls of men than any other event in human history." --John G. Lake
➢ "God proved His love on the Cross. When Christ hung, and bled, and died, it was God saying to the world, 'I love you." --Billy Graham

17. Salvation

The study of salvation is called "soteriology" (*soteria in Greek = salvation; logia in Greek = discourse*). Soteriology specifically refers to the study of the work of Christ in restoring lost men to God. Soteriology includes study of repentance, faith, election, justification, conversion, regen-eration, adoption, sanctification, and glorification. This study will focus on salvation in general.

God desires all men to be saved (I Tim 2:3-4). He sent Jesus to earth to preach the gospel and die for our sins (John 1:1-14; 3:16; Rom 3:25; Phil 2:5-8; I John 2:2; 4:10). Jesus is the source (author) of eternal salvation to those who obey Him (Heb. 5:9; cf. Heb. 12:2). People who confess Jesus as their personal Savior and Lord will go to heaven (Heb. 5:9; Rev. 22:14). But, people who do not confess Jesus as Savior and Lord will be cast into the lake of fire (Rev. 20:15) and be eternally separated from God (II Thess 1:8-9).

If we confess Jesus before men, He will confess us before His Father and the angels. But if we deny Jesus before men, He will deny us (Matt. 10:32-33; Luke. 12:8-9). The apostle Paul says that if we confess with our mouth that Jesus is Lord and believe in our hearts that God raised Him from the dead, we will be saved (Rom 10:9). Because, with our hearts we believe, resulting in righteousness, and with our mouth, we confess resulting in salvation (Rom.10:10).

Nine examples of conversion in the Bible
  1. Day of Pentacost (Acts 2:5-27)
  2. Samaritans (Acts 8:4-13)
  3. Ethiopian Eunuch (Acts 8:26-40)
  4. Paul (Acts 9:1-20; 22:16)
  5. Cornelius (Acts 10:34-48)
  6. Lydia (Acts 16:13-15)
  7. Philippian Jailer (Acts 16:25-34)
  8. Crispus, Corinthians (Acts 18:8)
  9. Ephesians (Acts 19:1-7)

God's Plan of Salvation
There are many "tracts" around that explain God's plan of salvation. Billy Graham's "Steps to Peace with God" has four steps. Bill Bright through Campus Crusade for Christ has the "Four Spiritual Laws". The Southern Baptist Convention publishes "Saved and Sure". Others have minor variations to the four steps—
  1. God loves you, offers a wonderful plan for your life, and wants you to experience peace and a meaningful purposeful life—abundant and eternal (Rom 5:1; John 3:16; John 10:10).
  2. Man is sinful, man chooses to disobey God and go his own way. This results in separation from God and, therefore, man cannot know and experience God's love and plan for his life (Rom 3:23; Rom 6:23; Prov 14:12; Isa 59:2)
  3. Jesus Christ is God's only provision for man's sin. He died on a cross and rose from the grave, paying the penalty for our sins and bridging the gap between God and man. Through Jesus you can know and experience God's love and plan for your life (I Tim 2:5; Rom 5:8; John 14:6; I Peter 3:18; I Cor 15:3-6)
  4. Each person individually must trust and receive Jesus Christ as Savior and Lord. Then you can know and experience God's love and plan for your life (John 1:12; Eph 2:8-9; John 3:1-8; Rom 10:9; Rev 3:20).

A Typical Prayer of Salvation
Dear God, I know that I am a sinner who deserves an eternal death. I desire to turn from my sin, but I know that on my own, I can never achieve a sinless life. Left on my own I will be forever separated from You. I

believe that Jesus Christ died and rose again as an eternal sacrifice for my sin. I accept the gift of Jesus and ask Him into my life as my Savior. Amen

If this was prayed with a sincere heart, you are from this very moment His Child (John 1:12). You have the assurance of His Word that you are truly saved from your sins and will have eternal life (Rom 10:13, I John 5:12-13). The Bible promises that the moment you receive Christ by faith as an act of your own free will, the following will happen: Christ will enter your life (Col 1:17, Rev 3:20), your sinful nature is forgiven (Col 1:14), you are now a child of God (John 1:12), you have eternal life (John 5:24), and you have begun the great adventure for which God created you (John 10:10; II Cor 5:17; I Thess 5:18).

What It Costs Not To Be A Christian? (1)
1. The sacrifice of peace—peace of conscience and peace of heart (Rom 5:1).
2. The sacrifice of joy—the highest, purest, truest, most satisfying and most enduring joy that is to be found on the earth (I Peter 1:7-8).
3. The sacrifice of hope (Titus 1:2).
4. The sacrifice of the highest manhood and womanhood—to glorify God (Rom 3:23)
5. The sacrifice of God's favor (John 3:36)
6. The sacrifice of Christ's acknowledgement in the world to come (Matt 10:32-33)
7. The sacrifice of eternal life—instead will perish forever (John 3:14-15)

The Five "P's" of Salvation
1. Pardon
2. Peace
3. Power
4. Purpose
5. Provision

"Salvation means certainty, security, and peace of mind"—Billy Graham

The letters of the word "gospel" appear in this order in John 3:16—For God so loved the world that He gave His only begotten Son, that whoever believes in Him shall not perish but have eternal life.

Discuss the following Scriptures and their teaching on salvation:
- Psalm 27
- Psalm 85:4-7
- Acts 4:10-12
- Rom 1:16
- Phil 2:12-13

Perpetual Questions About Salvation
1. Can a person lose his/her salvation?
2. What about those who died never knowing about Christ?
3. What about babies/young children who died without knowing the gospel?
4. What about those who love God, but did not accept Christ as Savior (e.g. the Jews)?
5. If a person rejects the message of salvation, will he/she really be doomed to hell?

Quotes
➢ "The greatest enemy to human souls is the self-righteous spirit which makes men look to themselves for salvation".—Charles Spurgeon
➢ "Three things are necessary for the salvation of man: to know what he ought to believe; to know what he ought to desire; and to know what he ought to do." -- Saint Thomas Aquinas

18. Confession and Repentance

What is the meaning of confession? How is confession different from repentance?

Confession and repentance are both involved in salvation. <u>Confession</u> means to acknowledge as being true, and <u>repentance</u> means to change one's heart and mind (1).

The Greek word "omologeœ" ("acknowledge, confess") is, literally, "say the same thing." If we say the same thing about our sins as God does, namely, that our sins are truly sinful; and if we have the kind of godly sorrow that leads to repentance (II Cor. 7:10-11); then the blood, by which is meant the bloody sacrificial death of Jesus continually purifies us from all sin.

Confession is to acknowledge one's guilt for sin and need of forgiveness. Confession is simply "owning" our negative thoughts and emotions and acknowledging that what we have thought or done, either ignorantly or knowingly, has quenched God's Spirit in us. Because it is sin, we must, therefore, confess "ownership" of it. Discuss I John 1:8-2:1

Repentence is the Greek word μετάνοια (metanoia), "after/behind one's mind", which is a compound word of the preposition 'meta' (after, with), and the verb 'noeo' (the result of perceiving or observing). In this compound word 'meta' combines the two meanings of time and change, so that the whole compound means: 'to think differently after'. Metanoia is therefore primarily an after-thought, different from the former thought; a change of mind accompanied by regret and change of conduct, "change of mind and heart", or, "change of consciousness". One of the key descriptions of repentance in the New Testament is the parable of the prodigal son (Luke 15).

Repentance involves the mind, emotions, and will - - the whole heart. It is not something done in a person's own strength. When a person listens responsively to the gospel message, the Holy Spirit enables him or her to repent (turn from sin) and have faith (turn to Christ). "For it is by grace you have been saved, through faith -- and this not from yourselves, it is the gift of God - - not by works, so that no one can boast" (Ephesians 2:8-9). The result of conversion is a new life of fellowship with God and growth into the likeness of Christ which will never end. – Billy Graham

Repentance is a change of mind resulting in a change of action. Repenting is simply choosing to turn around from following what our negative thoughts and emotions are telling us and, instead, choosing to follow whatever God has shown us. Repenting means we are to stop looking at and pointing to the other person and begin looking at and pointing to ourselves. We repent of our sins when we make the decision to change our lives to live in obedience to God. We no longer obey sin in its lusts (Rom. 6:12), but we obey God (Rom. 6:17; Heb. 5:9). We must repent before being baptized for the forgiveness of our sins (Acts 2:38). After being baptized, we must repent of sins we commit as God's children (Acts 8:22). Jesus commands us to repent. If we do not, we will perish (Luke 13:3, 5).

This critical step of confession and repentance is our <u>own </u>responsibility (Read 1 John 1:9). This is the step, however, that many of us have left out when we have given things over to the Lord. Certainly, we've given our hurts to God, but most of the time, we've forgotten to admit our own part in the problem. And this is why so many of the things we've surrendered to the Lord often do come back. If we don't do *our* part of confessing and repenting of our sin and self, God is hindered from doing His- taking our sins away "as far as the east is from the west (Psalm 103:12)." (2)

<u>The Danger of Failing to Repent (3)</u>
Instead of using Jesus' love as a way of dealing with our sins, we have used Him as an excuse to avoid dealing with our sins, which is quite a different thing. We are quick to identify sins in others. We mount

huge crusades to pluck splinters from other people's eyes, but we parade around with beams in our own. We are keenly perceptive of sins in other people, but we are blind to sins in our own souls. We are deaf to our own Scriptures condemning the hypocrites we have become!

Then we moan that no one takes us seriously. By not taking us seriously, worldly people demonstrate that, in some ways, they are more spiritually perceptive than we are.

Look at the hypocrisy we fall into when we fail to confess and repent. We become proud, where our Scriptures tell us to be humble (I Peter 5:5). We find mitigating factors for our own sins, but none for the sins of others (Luke 11:46). We think ourselves better than others, when clearly we are not (Philippians 2:3). We seek to be masters of others, instead of servants of all (Mark 9:35). We complain about hardship, when we are supposed to endure it joyfully (James 1:2). We conveniently overlook the fact that I John was written as a manual for Christians, not as a brochure to prospective converts.

What Do The Following Scriptures Teach About Confession and/or Repentance and What True Repentance Really Means?
- Psalm 32:3-5
- Psalm 51
- Proverbs 28:13
- Matthew 10:32
- Luke 3:7-8
- Romans 10:9
- Romans 6:1-12
- I Cor 5:17
- Eph 1:4
- Eph 4:22-24
- Col 3:5-10
- I Tim 2:19b

The basics of inductive Bible study typically have 10 questions we should ask ourselves about a Bible passage we are reading. Addressing these questions enables us to move from Bible reading to Bible study. One of those questions is "Is there sin in my life for which confession and repentance is needed?

A Simple Prayer of Confession (substitute "I" for "we" in this public prayer)
Most merciful God, we confess that we have sinned against you in thought, word, and deed, by what we have done, and by what we have left undone. We have not loved you with our whole heart; we have not loved our neighbors as ourselves. We are truly sorry and we humbly repent. For the sake of your Son Jesus Christ, have mercy on us and forgive us; that we may delight in your will, and walk in your ways, to the glory of your Name. Amen. (4)

Quotes
➢ "True repentance has as its constituent elements not only grief and hatred of sin, but also an apprehension of the mercy of God in Christ. It hates the sin, and not simply the penalty; and it hates the sin most of all because it has discovered God's love." - William Mackergo Taylor
➢ "Repentance must be something more than mere remorse for sins: it comprehends a change of nature befitting heaven."- Lew Wallace
➢ "Unless we realize our sins enough to call them by name, it is hardly worth while to say anything about them at all. When we pray for forgiveness, let us say, "my temper," or "untruthfulness," or "pride," "my selfishness, my cowardice, indolence, jealousy, revenge, impurity." To recognize our sins, we must look them in the face and call them by their right names, however hard. Honesty in confession calls for definiteness in confession."- Maltbie Davenport Babcock

19. Forgiveness

Forgiveness includes both God forgiving man and man forgiving other men.

<u>God's Forgiveness (1)</u>
"Without the shedding of Blood, there is no forgiveness" (Hebrews 9:22). In the Old Testament, the continual sacrifices of unblemished lambs were required to satisfy God's wrath and judgment. However, Jesus Christ, the Son of God, died on a Roman cross and became the ultimate, once-and-for-all sacrifice for our sins. Jesus purchased God's forgiveness on our behalf when he became the Lamb of God and died on the cross for you and me. A believer receives God's forgiveness when he repents of sin and places his faith in Jesus Christ for salvation -- all of his sins are forgiven forever (Col 2:13). That includes past, present and future, big or small. Jesus died to pay the penalty for all of our sins, and once they are forgiven, they are all forgiven. In Luke 4:18 Jesus said, "The Spirit of the Lord is upon me, because he hath anointed me to preach the gospel to the poor; he hath sent me to heal the brokenhearted, to preach deliverance (aphesis - forgiveness) to the captives, and recovering of sight to the blind, to set at liberty (aphesis - forgiveness) them that are bruised."

Read also: Psalm 32:1-2; Psalm 103:12; Psalm 130; Isa 43:25; Col 1:14; Acts 10:43; I John 1:8-9

<u>Meaning of Forgiveness</u>
Forgiveness is a complex emotional and spiritual process that touches many different levels of our existence. The dictionary defines the word "forgive" as doing three things:
1. To excuse for a fault or offense, i.e. to pardon--to forgive someone means that you have completely released and excused the person that hurt you. You have completely let it go.
2. To renounce anger or resentment against-- you have to cast down and disavow all internal feelings of anger or resentment that their offense may have caused you.
3. To absolve from payment of a debt-- you have to remove from your mind any expectation that the person that offended you will ever make things right.

In the New Testament the main word used to convey the idea of forgiveness is the Greek verb "aphiemi" and the noun "aphesis." These are compound words that come from the Greek "apo" which means off or away; and the Greek "hiemi" which means to send forth. New Testament word for forgiveness literally means to send forth or to send away. Both words are found a total of 163 times in the New Testament and are translated forgive, forsake, lay aside, let go, put away, remit, deliverance, remission, et al.

<u>Main Biblical References for Man's Need to Forgive (2)</u>
In Matt 6:12 Jesus taught the disciples to pray, "Father.... forgive us our debts, as we forgive our debtors." Jesus tied the amount of forgiveness that we receive from God to the amount of forgiveness that we give to others.
1. In Matt 6:14-15 He said, "For if you forgive men their debts your heavenly Father will also forgive you. But if you forgive not men their debts, neither will your Father forgive your debts." This is an extraordinary and powerful statement that is of great significance for the believer. If you refuse to forgive others you will not be forgiven by God. It you hold on to unforgiveness it will severely restrict your life in God. You will never become the free, anointed, blessed child of God that you desire to be if you allow thoughts of resentment and anger to remain in your heart. You must learn how to let go of the trespasses that others have committed against you if you want to be a successful and healthy Christian.
2. Psalm 86:5—God is always willing and ready to forgive
3. Matt 18:21-22—Jesus' model of forgiveness
4. Luke 23:34-- Jesus' example of forgiveness
5. Eph 4:32—commandment for us to forgive one another

Main Benefits of Forgiveness
1. It is necessary for our own forgiveness. (Mark 11:25, 26)
2. It restores Christian fellowship. (2 Cor 2:5–10)
3. Spiritual cleansing. (James 5:15-16)
4. Real Christians, the people that have truly allowed the Lord to change their lives, do not spread strife. They don't stir up conflict. They have trained themselves to be quick to forgive others. They have disciplined their hearts and their minds to quickly let hurt feelings go.

Examples of Forgiveness:
- Esau and Jacob. (Gen 33:4–15)
- Joseph (Gen 45:8–15)
- Moses (Num 12:1–13)
- David (II Sam 19:18–23)
- Solomon (II Kings 1:52, 53)
- Jesus (Luke 23:34)
- Stephen (Acts 7:59-60)
- Paul (II Tim 4:16)

The Problems of Unforgiveness
1. Gives Satan opportunities--In II Cor 2:11 the Apostle Paul admonishes us to, "...forgive....lest Satan should get an advantage of us; for we are not ignorant of his devices." The devil will take advantage of every instance of resentment and bitterness that you allow to stay in your heart; and he will viciously use it against you. Refusing to forgive, will open the doors of your life to satanic activity. He who cannot forgive cannot love (see also I Peter 4:8)
2. Hindered prayer – Mark 11:25 --"...forgive him and let it drop (leave it, let it go), in order that your Father Who is in heaven may also forgive you your own failings and shortcomings and let them drop." (Amplified). Jesus said that God will not be able to forgive you if you can't find a way to forgive others. This is also implied in the Lord's Prayer. Many in the body of Christ feel frustrated and defeated in life because their prayers seem to go unanswered. But the reality is, they have obstructed their relationship with God by allowing bitterness and resentment (hurt feelings) to stay in their heart towards someone that has offended them.
3. Lack of peace--thoughts of unforgiveness, bitterness or resentment make you a prisoner to strife, governed by anger, and a captive to hate. Unforgiveness robs joy and peace right out of your heart.

Questions
1. What kind of offense do you find most difficult to forgive?
2. Do you meditate on an offense over and over?
3. How do you find it in yourself to let go of past offenses
4. Does forgiving someone mean that the offense is forgotten and has no further consequences?
5. What is the only phrase in the Lord's prayer with a "condition" attached? (Matt 6:12)

Quotes
- "The weak can never forgive. Forgiveness is the attribute of the strong."—Gandhi
- "There is no revenge so complete as forgiveness."—Josh Billings
- "He that cannot forgive others, breaks the bridge over which he himself must pass if he would reach heaven; for everyone has the need to be forgiven"—Thomas Fuller
- "Forgiveness is man's deepest need and highest achievement" -- Horace Bushnell

20. Purpose of Life

In my opinion there is no finer Christian book written than Rick Warren's "Purpose-Driven Life" (1) The following are my notes taken from his book.

<u>God's Five Purposes For Our Lives—in order to bring glory to God</u>
"Most people struggle with three basic issues in life. The first is identity: 'Who am I? The second is importance: 'Do I matter?' The third is impact: 'What I my place in life?' The answers to all three questions are found in God's five purposes for you.

Purpose Number	Focus of Purpose	What God Did?	Who Am I?	What Must I Do	Question I Must Answer	Answering This Question	Scrip-ture
1	Worship	I was planned for God's pleasure	Magnifier of His glory	Love God with all your heart	What will be the center of my life?	Helps me focus on God	Isa 61:13
2	Fellowship	I was formed for God's family	Member of His family	Baptize them into	What will be the community of my life?	Helps me face life's problems	John 15:5
3	Disciple-ship	I was created to become like Christ	Model of His character	Teach them to do	What will be the character of my life?	Helps fortify my faith	Col 2:7
4	Ministry	I was shaped for serving God	Minister of His grace	Love your neighbor	What will be the contri-bution of my life?	Helps me find my talents	I Cor 3:5-6
5	Mission	I was made for a mission	Messenger of God's good news	Go and make disciples	What will be the commu-nication of my life?	Helps fulfill my mission	Prov 11:30

<u>Some Of The Best Thoughts From The Book</u>
God's view of life: Life is a <u>test</u>; a <u>trust</u>; a <u>temporary assignment</u> (p.42)

God created the church to meet your five deepest needs in life--<u>Purpose</u> to live for; <u>People</u> to live with; <u>Principles</u> to live by; <u>Profession</u> to live out; and <u>Power</u> to live on (p.136)

Characteristics of biblical fellowship--Authenticity (share our true feelings); Mutuality (encourage one another); Sympathy (support each other); Mercy (forgive each other); Honesty (speak the truth in love); Humility (admit our weaknesses); Courtesy (respect our differences); Confidentiality (not gossip); Frequency (make group a priority) (p.151)

God uses His Word (the truth we need to grow), people (the support we need to grow), and circumstances (the environment we need to practice Christlikeness) to mold us. (p.176)

Five factors that make up our capabilities—**SHAPE**-- **S**piritual gifts, **H**eart, **A**bilities, **P**ersonality, **E**xperience (p.236)

<u>Some of the 40 Questions We Are Asked to Ponder</u>
- How can I remind myself that life is really about living for God, not myself? (Col 1:16b)
- Knowing that God uniquely created me, what areas of my personality, background, and physical appearance am I struggling to accept? (Isa 44:2)
- What would my family and friends say is the driving force of my life? What do I want it to be? (Isa 26:3)

- Since I was made to last forever, what is the one thing I should stop doing and the one thing I should start doing today? (I John 2:17)
- What has happened to me recently that I now realize was a test from God? What are the greatest matters God has entrusted to me? (Luke 16:10a)
- How should the fact that life on earth is just a temporary assignment change the way I am living (II Cor 4:18)
- Where in my daily routine can I become more aware of God's glory? (Romans 11:36)
- Since God knows what is best, in what areas of my life do I need to trust Him most? (Psalm 147:11)
- What area of my life am I holding back from God? (Romans 6:13b)
- How can I remind myself to think about God and talk to Him more often throughout the day? (Ps 25:14a)
- What practical choices will I make today in order to grow closer to God? (James 4:8a)
- How can I stay focused on God's presence, especially when He feels distant? (Hebrews 15:5)
- How can I start treating other believers like members of my own family? (Eph 1:5a)
- Honestly, are relationships my first priority? How can I ensure that they are? (Gal 5:14)
- What one step can I take today to connect with another believer at a more heart-to-heart level? (Gal 6:2)
- How can I help cultivate the characteristics of real community in my small group and my church? (I Jn 3:16)
- Who do I need to restore a broken relationship with today? (Romans 12:18)
- What I am personally doing to protect unity in my church family right now? (Romans 14:19)
- In what area of my life do I need to ask for the Spirit's power to be like Christ today? (II Cor 3:18b)
- What is one area where I need to stop thinking my way and start thinking God's way? (Romans 12:2b)
- What has God already told me in His Word that I haven't started doing yet? (John 8:31-32)
- What problem in my life has caused the greatest growth in me? (Romans 8:28)
- What Christlike character quality can I develop by defeating the most common temptation I face? (Jam 1:12)
- Who could I ask to be a spiritual partner to help me defeat a persistent temptation by praying for me? (I Cor 10:13b)
- In what area of my spiritual growth do I need to be more patient and persistent? (Phil 1:6)
- In what way can I see myself passionately serving others and loving it? (I Cor 12:6)
- What God-given ability or personal experience can I offer to my church? (I Peter 4:10)
- Which of the six characteristics of real servants offers the greatest challenge to me? (Matt 10:42)
- Am I limiting God's power in my life by trying to hide my weaknesses? What do I need to be honest about in order to help others? (II Cor 12:9a)
- What fears have kept me from fulfilling the mission God made me to accomplish? What keeps me from telling others the Good News: (Matthew 28:19-20)
- As I reflect on my personal story, who does God want me to share it with? (I Peter 3:15b-15)
- What steps can I take to prepare to go on a short-term missions experience in the next year? (Ps 67:2)
- When will I take the time to write down my answers to life's five great questions? When will I put my purpose on paper? (Acts 13:36)

Quotes
- "You were made by God and for God—and until you understand that, life will never make sense." (p. 18)
- "First, What did you do with my Son, Jesus? Second, What did you do with what I gave you? The first question will determine where you spend eternity. The second question will determine what you do in eternity." (p. 34)
- "In order to keep us from becoming too attached to earth, God allows us to feel a significant amount of discontent and dissatisfaction in life—longings that will never be fulfilled on this side of eternity. We're not completely happy here because we're not supposed to be!" (p. 50)
- "If you fail to fulfill your God-given mission on earth, you will have wasted the life God gave you." (p. 285)

21. Victory in Life

Key verse: I Cor 15:57-58: "But thanks be to God, who gives us the victory through our Lord Jesus Christ. Therefore, my beloved brethren, be steadfast, immovable, always abounding in the work of the Lord, knowing that your toil is not in vain in the Lord."

I Cor 15:57-58 (1)

I want you to notice that is put in the present tense. It is not past, "who gave us the victory." I do not know anything that means more to me as a Christian than the fact that every day I can lay hold of the grace of Jesus Christ. He is not a distant Savior who lived twenty centuries ago. He is alive, and I meet him every day. When I find myself having failed, faltered, and sinned, I come again and receive from him the cleansing that he has won for me on Calvary. That gives me new power to say, "No!" to all the evil, afflictions, and pressures of my life. I know that *that* evil is put away; it will never come back to haunt me; I will not have to face it at the judgment seat of God. That is why this passage ends with Verse 58: When you go back to your work do not see it as simply a way by which you earn your living. It has been given to you as an opportunity for you to have a ministry in which you witness, you demonstrate a changed life, a heart at peace, the radiant joy of fellowship with a living Lord on your face, and love pouring out of your heart to those who, like you, have struggled and lost frequently in the rat race of life. That is what God sends us out to do as Christians. He has given us a work, not that we might make notable achievements which men applaud, and in which we make a name for ourselves. What God looks for is how are we behaving towards others? How do we show a loving spirit, a gracious, forgiving attitude, a willingness to return good for evil, an ability to speak a word of release to those who are prisoners of their own habits, to set free those who are oppressed by wrong, hateful attitudes, to bind up the brokenhearted, and to open the eyes of the blind? That is the work of the Lord.

As Christians, we can claim victory over any kind of adversary or problem in our lives. Here are some examples:

Victory Over Temptation (James 4:17)
- Jesus was tempted like us (Matt 4:1-11; Heb 2:18; Heb 4:15) so He understands our temptations and can/will help us (Christians) defeat them (II Peter 2:9).
- Remember the promise that we are never tempted beyond what we are able to overcome (I Cor 10:13)

Victory Over Sin (Romans 3:33; 6:23)
- Yes, we all have sinned—sin nature (Rom 3:23) and still sin (I John 1:8-2:1), but we can overcome the penalty of sin through Jesus (Eph 1:7; I Peter 1:18-20)
- This victory also helps us to deal with the guilt over sin that otherwise could linger and keep us from moving forward (Ps 38:4-8). Some try to overcome sin by denying their own personal guilt, but again, only through Jesus can we truly overcome sin.
- Eph 6:10-18 describes how to be victorious over sin and temptation

Victory Over the World (I John 5:4-5)
- It is our faith in Jesus that enables us to overcome what the world can do to bring us down (John 16:33; I John 5:4-5)
- I John 2:15-16 reminds us not to love the world or the things in the world
- There is a price to pay when we choose not to follow what the world tempts us to do (John 15:18-19)

Victory Overcoming Suffering

- We know that sorrow, pain, suffering, troubles are an indisputable fact of human existence. As Christians, the Bible says to expect suffering since Jesus Himself suffered (Heb 5:8-10). The road of life is generally hard and uphill. (Job 14:1; John 16:33)
- Paul regarded Jesus Christ as the Source of consolation and affirmed that the comfort which He imparts is more than sufficient to over balance all the sorrow which he would have to suffer (II Cor 1:3-5; I Thess 4:13).
- The Christian attitude in facing and overcoming suffering is described in Romans 8:18 and 8:28.
- Psalm 20 is subtitled "Prayer for Victory Over Enemies"

Victory Over Death

- Most of I Cor 15 describes this victory
- See also John 5:28-29 and John 11:25-26

Questions

1. How can you overcome your fear of death?
2. Describe some of your victories as a Christian.
3. Describe a victorious life…..who might serve as an example?
4. What do you need to do to claim a victorious life?
5. Is a victorious life the same as a prosperous life?

"The Thinking Christian" (2)

As a Christian are you going to live a victorious life? In a manner of speaking, yes. Our victory is Christ's death on the cross which defeated the sting of death. A victorious life is not success, prosperity, or happiness but freedom from the condemnation of sin and the availability of the Holy Spirit to power a Christ-like life. Because of His victory we are free to grow and mature and prosper spiritually. So, does that mean God wants us to suffer in poverty and abuse? Of course not, God loves us and hurts to see us suffer. That's why we have the church, our fellow Christians, and the promise of His imminent return. What do you think?

Quotes

➢ "There are no victories without conflicts, no rainbow without a cloud and a storm"—Unknown
➢ "The smile of God is victory." –John Greenleaf Whittier
➢ "A victory won over self, is the only victory acceptable to God."--Charles Nelson Douglas

22. Discipleship

What is Discipleship?
The word "disciple" in the Greek is "mathetes" meaning "learner". A disciple of Jesus Christ is a person who follows the teaching of Christ. A lack of personal commitment to Christ is the greatest problem of the church. If you claim to be a Christian then Jesus Christ Himself has given you several specific commands to obey and follow—Luke 9:23; Luke 14:25-35; Matt 10:38; John 8:31-32; John 15:7-8. Let's look closer at a couple of these--

Luke 9:23 (or Matt 10:38) (1)
1. What is the call to consider?
    ▪ Why would anyone wish to come after Christ? What does He offer? Certainty, security, peace of mind
    ▪ To follow Jesus, to trust in Him, to grow to experience the abundant new life in Him
    ▪ We are called to overcome mediocrity, to live differently, to soar in life
        - A life that soars is a life that does not get caught in the trap of the temporal.
        - A life that soars does not quit, does not allow life's circumstances to push them down
        - A life that soars models a high level of excellence, excellence that has resulted from a mind that thinks like Christ (Rom 12:1-2; II Cor 10:5)

2. What are the conditions to be met?
    ▪ How do you deny yourself?
        - This is NOT self-rejection or not enjoying life. It is to deny everything rooted in the old life (Read I John 2:15-16). It is the "brutal setting aside of pride and fear and all the rights that the old self demands as its due"
        - Give an example of where you have denied yourself (e.g. forgiveness, service, overcoming lust and pride, etc.)
    ▪ How do you take up your cross?
        - This is not the cross of Christ. Jesus' cross was crucifixion and terrible suffering, that was God's will for Him.
        - Your cross is to choose as Jesus did, to do whatever God wants you to do.
        - What is your cross?

3. What is the choice to make?
    ▪ To keep close to Christ or follow our own way
    ▪ To choose Christ enables one to live powerfully and triumphantly to do God's will, thus denying the old self.

Luke 14:25-35. The choice to be a disciple of Christ affects (1):
1. Our personal relationships
    ▪ Commitment involves reorienting your relationships
    ▪ Commitment to Jesus demands full participation

2. Our personal goals and desires
    ▪ Commitment involves re-orienting your plans and goals
    ▪ You must give us selfish desires
    ▪ Like training for the Olympics, training in the military, obtaining degrees and certifications, discipleship requires endless hours of constant, painful repetition

3. Our personal possessions
    ▪ Commitment involves a willingness to pay the price
    ▪ What price do you need to pay to be a true disciple?

"The Conditions of Discipleship" from Luke 14:26, 27, 33 (2)

"If the closest relationships of a disciple's life conflict with the claims of Jesus Christ, then our Lord requires instant obedience to Himself. Discipleship means personal, passionate devotion to Jesus. To be a disciple is to be a devoted bondservant motivated by love for the Lord Jesus. No one on earth has a passionate love for the Lord Jesus unless the Holy Spirit has given it to him. The Christian life is a life characterized by true and spontaneous creativity. Consequently, a disciple is subject to the same charge that was leveled against Jesus Christ, namely, the charge of inconsistency. But Jesus was always consistent in his relationship to God, and a Christian must be consistent in his relationship to the life of the Son of God in him, not consistent to strict, unyielding doctrines."

Five Reasons Why Christians Fail To Be Disciples
1. Lack of spiritual understanding
2. Lack of humility
3. Lack of faith
4. Lack of commitment
5. Lack of power

How can a person overcome the above failures if he or she desires to be a true follower of Jesus Christ and receive His promises and blessings?
1. Be certain that you have a personal relationship with Jesus Christ that you have specifically invited Him to live in your heart (Rev 3:20; John 15:5)
2. Bible study, Bible study, Bible study!!! Studying and mediating on (not just reading) the Bible is the only way a Christian can grow spiritually. The Bible itself claims to be THE source of truth, joy, victory, faith, power, guidance, and growth (II Tim 3:16-17; Rom 10:17; I Peter 2:2; Psalm 119:105).
3. Pray every day (Phil 4:6-7; I Thess 5:17)
4. Fellowship with other Christians (Heb 10:24-25)
5. Be a Christian steward: Service, Giving, Witnessing, Obeying (Mark 12:30-31; II Cor 9:6-8; Matt 5:13-16; John 14:21)

A true disciple of Christ will then have the ability to make an impact on other people's lives in a positive way for Christ. Such people usually have the following four characteristics: Consistency, Authenticity, Unselfishness, and Tirelessness.

Questions
1. What stands have you taken for Christ?

2. What sacrifices have you made for Christ and others?

3. How much of your day do you devote serving Christ and others?

Quotes
➤ "At the back of it there lies the central citadel of obstinacy: I will not give up my right to myself--the thing God intends you to give up if ever you are going to be a disciple of Jesus Christ" --Oswald Chambers
➤ "Christianity without discipleship is always Christianity without Christ." --Dietrich Bonhoeffer (Note: He wrote the classic book "The Cost of Discipleship", 1937).

23. Righteousness and Holiness

What is the real meaning of "righteousness" and "holiness" and what is the difference between these two Christian qualities? Scripture distinguishes holiness and righteousness as being two very distinguishable qualities in Christian experience. For example, Eph 4:24: "…..and put on a new self, which in the likeness of God has been created in righteousness and holiness of the truth". (1)

HOLINESS: The Vertical Pursuit (relationship with God)
- The Greek word for holiness is *hagiasmos* --denotes a moral nature in pursuit of God's likeness, i.e., godliness, or the state of possessing a nature of holy character befitting those who profess godliness.
- This speaks of a nature given us by God at the time of new birth (justification) and which we continue to cultivate and perfect as holiness is pursued, and so long as we remain in obedience, or in *"the way"*. (Matt 7:14; Acts 16:17; 18:25; 2 Peter 2:15,21)
- Keeping the mind upon God, carrying His presence, pleasing Him, fearing Him and reverencing Him in all things. It is to hold His Word in high regard. It embraces the virtues of prayer, meditation and the practice of His presence. (Isa 26:3; 2 Cor 7:1; Phil 2:12)
- Holiness is UNTO THE LORD and not unto man. It cares only to please God, not caring what men may think. (Exo 28:36)

RIGHTEOUSNESS: The horizontal pursuit (relationship with other people)
- The Greek word for righteousness is *dikaiosune*; to deal justly and honestly with others.
- Manifests itself in the form of good manners, being fair, courteous and thoughtful of others.
- Righteousness is unto all men. It is vicarious living (for others). It does matter that men see us as considerate, kind and thoughtful toward their well being. All of God's commandments teach consideration of others. (Matt 5:16; Eph 5:21)

Holiness	Righteousness
Our relationship with God	Our relationship with other people
Learned only from God	Can be learned from other people
Our devotion to God	My responsibility toward other people
Treating God as He likes to be treated	Treating people as they like to be treated
Essential to divine government	Essential to human government
Produces personal perfection	Produces social order
Our personal experience with God that affects my right relationship with people	Our right experience with people born out of our right relationship with God

Notice how these two words are used together as two different qualities in the Christian life:
- Luke 1:74-75 - "That he would grant unto us, that we being delivered out of the hand of our enemies might serve him without fear, in holiness [*hosiotes*; piety] and righteousness [*dikaiosune*] before him, all the days of our life."
- Romans 6:19 - "I speak after the manner of men because of the infirmity of your flesh: for as you have yielded your members servants to uncleanness and to iniquity unto iniquity; even so now yield your members servants to righteousness (*dikaiosune*) unto holiness (*hagiosmos*)."
- I Cor 1:30 - "But of him are you in Christ Jesus, who of God is made unto us wisdom, and righteousness (*dikaiosune*), and sanctification (*hagiasmos*), and redemption:"
- I Tim 6:11 - "But you, O man of God, flee these things; and follow after righteousness, (*dikaiosune*) godliness (*Eusebeia*), piety, devoutness, devotion, holiness, faith, love, patience, meekness.

True Righteousness and Holiness (2)

There are the only three verses where the terms righteousness and holiness appear together in the same verse in the Scriptures. Eph 4:24 is where we see that we who are in Christ have been transformed and made new. And the new man that we are is created in right relationship to God, meeting His standards because of the imputed righteousness of Christ.

The second verse is Luke 1:75. This is the prophecy of Zacharias, John the Baptist's father. In this prophecy he states that the Messiah is coming so that His people might serve God. This service is done without fear for perfect love casts our fear. And this service is done in holiness and righteousness all the days of our life. Because Christ has come we are now able to serve God without fear in holiness and righteousness.

The third verse is Rom 6:19 where we learn that we have been freed from sin and are now slaves of righteousness. And it is said that we are slaves of righteousness for holiness. That is, where we once we ruled by sin now we are ruled by righteousness so that we are able to be holy! And all of this flows as a free gift from God through the salvation provided us in Christ Jesus.

We see then that everything we are as a followers of Christ points us and others to Christ! If you claim to be a Christian then your life must point others to Christ. There is no attention drawn to self for our accomplishments of good, righteousness, and holiness. Instead we "let our light shine" before men by being righteous and being holy as Christ lives in us! We cannot be right with God on our own. We cannot be holy on our own. So God has created us anew, transforming us from darkness to light, adopting us as sons and daughters, and through His Son making us right and pleasing to Him. All of that to say this - the Christian life, if true, always points to Christ.

Questions for Discussion
1. It has been said that there is no such thing as holiness in man without a prayer life. Do you agree? Why? (Read James 5:16)
2. Jesus says that His people are to hunger and thirst for righteousness (Matt 5:6). Matthew Henry says about this verse: "Those who hunger and thirst after righteousness are happy. Righteousness produces spiritual blessings. These are purchased for us by the righteousness of Christ, confirmed by the faithfulness of God. Our desires of spiritual blessings must be earnest. Such desires are from God, and He will not forsake the work of his own hands." Discuss this statement by Jesus and one explanation by a famous commentator.
3. The holiness of man is the state of being morally perfected (I Peter 1:15-16). Note that we are not as holy as He is, but we are called to be like Him in holiness. What are examples of being holy like God is holy?
4. What do the following passages teach about righteousness and holiness:
   a. Psalm 1—how the righteous and the wicked are contrasted
   b. Psalm 73—the end of the wicked contrasted with what happens with the righteous.
   c. Psalm 96—the Lord will judge the world in righteousness
   d. Matt 6:33—discuss Jesus' emphasis on seeking God's righteousness
   e. Heb 12:10-11—How can God's discipline enable us to share His holiness? Think about what is the peaceful fruit of righteousness.
   f. Other familiar passages about righteousness and holiness: Ps 23:3; Prov 10 (13 promises); Hab 2:4; John 15:8,10; Rom 10:10; Rom 12:1; Col 1:21; I John 1:9.

Quotes
➤ "You can always tell when you are on the road of righteousness—it's uphill" – Ernest Blevins
➤ "True holiness consists in doing God's will with a smile" –Mother Teresa
➤ "Holiness, not happiness, is the chief end of man." –Oswald Chambers

24. Suffering and Persecution

Suffering and persecution are events that no one wishes to experience, yet we all do, absolutely no human being escapes it. Of all possible theological mysteries of life, the number one mystery and the number one question people have is "why does God allow suffering in this world?" Christians, especially, ask this question. While there is no completely satisfying answer, especially during the times that we are suffering, there are compelling reasons given in Scripture. Keep in mind, too, that all of God's heroes and heroines suffered, even His own Son!

The Bible indicates that the "seed" of suffering started when sin entered the world (Gen 3:16-19). Suffering was not part of God's original plan (Gen 1:31). Mankind brought suffering because of his rebellion against God. Yet, God has a way of bringing good out of evil.

Why Christians are not exempt from suffering?
1. We're human—we get ill, we have heartaches and can be victims of disasters, tragedies, and death.
2. We still sin and disobey God (Heb 12:5-11)
3. If Christians did not suffer, our faith would be viewed as a fallout shelter for millions of hypocrites
4. God uses suffering to discipline us (Rev 3:19, Heb 11:32-38)

Why Do People Suffer? (1)
❖ Suffering keeps the world from becoming too attractive. Woe to the man or woman whose life on earth is so pleasant that he/she forgets about heaven (I Peter 2:11).
❖ Suffering brings out our best. There are no petty differences when a family rallies around a loved one who is suffering.
❖ Suffering gives an occasion to put to silence the enemies of God. Everyone knows the story of Job and how that turned out. Those who know the Lord do not shy away from suffering or death.
❖ Suffering makes us appreciative. We receive so many good things, especially our health, that we take them for granted that can make us unappreciative of our true blessings.
❖ Suffering makes us depend on God. It all depends on God, it always does, but we seldom really acknowledge this. When the medical team says, "We've done all that we can do", then you understand that God is in control (Isaiah 54:5).
❖ Suffering purifies us. You will finally get completely truthful with God when it gets really bad (I Peter 4:12-19).
❖ Suffering makes us empathetic. Truly compassionate people have been there where the suffering is and/or has been (II Cor 1:3-6)
❖ Suffering makes one humble. Pride goes before the fall. Once you or a loved one is in the "slough of despond", prideful things fall away.
❖ Suffering teaches us to pray. The depths of our needs are proportional to the height with which we pray. Lying on one's face, arms stretched out to our Lord, this is genuine, heartfelt communication with the Almighty.

Responses to Suffering (2)
God uses suffering to purify us and prove us faithful so that we will reflect who He is to others. Our response to trials and difficulties should bring honor and glory to the Lord.
▪ Three main responses to suffering
  o Resentment toward/against God
  o Resignation—maybe spiritual, but not virtuous
  o Acceptance—Matt 11:28-30; Rom 5:3-5; James 1:2-4; Rom 8:18; II Tim 2:12
▪ During our suffering what are we specifically instructed to do? What knowledge enables us to

respond in this way? (James 1:2-8)
- What can you learn about the relationship of trials and faith? (I Peter 1:6-7)
- What does God promise to a believer when we go through trials and suffering? (Rom 5:1-5)
- What other promises are in the Bible to those who are suffering? (Note: there are over 8,000 promises, but here are a few)---
  o He is our shield (Deut 33:12, Psalm 91:4)
  o He is our refuge (Psalm 41:1-3, 46:1, 62:8)
  o He is our strength (Psalm 28:7, Phil 4:13)
  o He is our shepherd (Psalm 23, John 10;11-14)
  o He is interested in us and provides for us (Eph 3:16-21)
  o He will be present in our troubles (James 4:8)
  o He will supply whatever we need to endure (Phil 4:19)
  o His grace is sufficient during trouble (II Cor 12:9)
  o He is our God of all comfort (II Cor 1:3-6)
  o He will never allow any difficulty to enter our lives without His accompanying offers to help and reward us in the life to come (I Cor 10:13)

What we can do for others who are going through times of suffering
- Suffer with them—use our ears and our hearts-- (weep with those who weep—Rom 12:15)
- Bear one another's burdens share our time and possessions (Gal 6:2)
- Pray and use Scripture to share God's loving promises (James 5:13, 16)
- Those who have suffered make the best comforters (II Cor 1:4)
- We should help even those beyond our own social sphere (The Good Samaritan)

Persecution
Jesus and Paul stated several times that followers of Christ will be persecuted ("dioko" = to pursue, suffer). Why? Because the cross separates Christians from the world (John 15:18-21; 16:1-4, 17:14-18; II Tim 3:12)
- Great blessings promised for those who are persecuted for righteousness' sake (Matt 5:10-12; Rom 8:16-18; 8:35-39; II Cor 4:7-11; I Peter 3:14-15)
- Biblical responses to persecution: Psalm 31:16; Matt 5:43-45; Acts 5:28-29; Romans 12:14; I Peter 4:12-13
- Unbiblical responses to persecution (sin and compromise): Matt 13:18-23; Mark 8:38)
- Triumph through persecution: Phil 1:12-14

Quotes
- "Pain, God's megaphone, can drive me away from Him. I can hate God for allowing such misery. Or, it can drive me to Him"—Philip Yancey
- "People are not persecuted for doing wrong but for doing right" –Unknown
- "God will not look you over for medals, degrees, or diplomas, but for scars"—Unknown
- "Although the world is full of suffering, it is also full of the overcoming of it."—Helen Keller
- "Difficult times have helped me to understand better than before, how infinitely rich and beautiful life is in every way, and that so many things that one goes worrying about are of no importance whatsoever". -- Isak Dinesen
- "It is doubtful that God can use any many greatly until He has hurt him deeply"—AWTozer
- "It is possible to escape a multitude of trouble by living an insignificant life"—JH Jewett

25. Backsliding

Backsliding is turning away from God. Backsliding made an impact on me early in my Christian life. After re-dedicating my life to Christ when I was 28, I started attending an adult Bible study class and was so impressed with one of the men leaders of the group. He sang, taught, and even wrote poetry about the Christian life. One day he simply disappeared and I later learned that he left his wife for another woman and stopped serving the Lord. I was stunned yet learned that backsliding can happen to any Christian and we have to be on guard against this.

What Do We Mean By "Backsliding"? (1,2)

Backsliding was first described in I Kings 11:9 that describe Solomon turning away from God. Backsliding is also described in Rev 2:4 as growing cold and leaving your first love. Backsliding is when a person who follows Christ turns away from Him. To the backslider, God is no longer the main focus of his life. Without God's leading, the person suffers a lapse morally and reverts back to sin. He "backslides" into his old way of life. The backslider no longer has interest in the Bible, in prayer, in church attending, in witnessing, and prefers turning back to the world. Think about what Jesus said in Luke 9:62.

What Causes Us To Backslide?

Backsliding is a gradual process. Little things creep into our lives and eventually undermine our faith. Lot in Genesis is an example of this graduate process.

- He started coveting worldly things—Gen 13:10
- He chose too low—to live in the plain instead of on the mountain—Gen 13:11
- He compromised his life by pitching his tent toward Sodom—Gen 13:12-13
- He was eventually captured by the enemy by flirting with it—Gen 14:11-12
- He became carnal—he loved Sodom—Gen 19:1,16
- He developed criminal weakness by giving his own daughters into sin—Gen 19:8
- He developed a love toward carousing—Gen 19:33-38

Pride can be found at the root of backsliding. Pride tells us we don't need God to lead us. Pride takes two forms when it comes to backsliding: Trying to justify oneself to God and taking part in sin. Always be on guard against the subtle attacks/influences of pride (Prov 16:18, I Cor 10:12).

Trying To Justify Oneself Leads To Backsliding

In Gal 5:4, Paul tells us that trying to justify oneself through the law (or through good deeds) can lead to backsliding. How can doing a good deed cause backsliding? Well, let's say someone helps an elderly woman across the street. The Christian who is walking with God will say, "Jesus has been kind to me so I want to be kind to others." Whereas the Christian who is backsliding will say, "I am acceptable to God because I helped this woman across the street." Pride makes the backslider think that he can impress God when in reality he is moving away from Him because, "God opposes the proud but gives grace to the humble" (James 4:6).

Taking Part In Sin Leads To Backsliding

Read Gal 5:13. Pride makes the backslider say, "I can lead my own life. I don't need God to tell me what to do." Less and less time is spent looking for God's direction. The backslider will stop praying and reading the Bible. Without God's direction the backslider will -- without even realizing it -- lead himself. This results in a sinful life away from God. Always be aware of what Jesus said in John 15:5. Pride results in a gradual failure to maintain a quiet time, pray, read the Bible, attend church, obey the Holy Spirit, confess Christ, and walk in the light of the Lord.

What Happens When We Backslide?

When we no longer seek the Lords leading, we will lack direction. When we no longer seek fellowship with Him, our hearts will become empty (Isa 59:9-10). This is because you and I were created to follow the Lord. We were created to have a relationship with God. And as terrible as it is to have never have known the love of Jesus Christ, how much worse is it to have experienced it and then turn away? Once you've followed Jesus nothing else can ever truly satisfy you. Also backsliding will lead to loss of rewards in the afterlife (I Cor 3:15). This is why backsliding is such a terrible thing. You try to replace His prefect love with something inferior. But the Lord stretches out His hand to you and offers to forgive your backsliding and restore you (Jer 3:12, 3:22).

How Do We Overcome Backsliding?
If you have found yourself backsliding, or drifting away from the Lord, these practical steps will help get you back on course today.
1. Examine your faith-life regularly—II Cor 13:5
2. If you find yourself drifting away, turn back immediately—Heb 3:12-13
3. Come to God daily for forgiveness and cleansing—I John 1:9, Rev 22:14
4. Continue daily seeking the Lord with your whole heart—I Chron 28:9
5. Stay in the Word of God; keep studying and learning daily—Prov 4:13
6. Stay in fellowship often with other believers. You can't make it alone as a Christian. We need the strength and prayers of other believers—Heb 10:25
7. Stand firm in your faith. Expect difficult times in your Christian life—Matt 10:22, Gal 5:1
8. Persevere—I Tim 4:15-17
9. Run the race to win—I Cor 9:24-25, II Tim 4:7-8
10. Remind yourself of what God has done for you in the past—Heb 10:32, 35-39

If you know that you are backsliding, pray the prayer from Isa 59:12. God will forgive you (II Chron 7:14) and restore you (Hos 14:4) and give you peace (Isa 57:19)

Quotes
➤ "Collapse in the Christian life is seldom a blowout; it is usually a slow leak" –Paul E. Little
➤ "Backsliding begins when knee-bending ends" –Unknown
➤ "A wrong sum can be put right, but only by going back till you find the error and working it afresh from that point, never by simply going on."—C.S. Lewis

26. Prophecy and The Second Coming of Christ

The Second Coming of Jesus Christ is the greatest single theme in Scripture (1). The main theme of the Bible is the Lord Jesus Christ, and the main subject is the Kingdom that His Father has promised Him. While there are approximately three hundred prophecies in the Old Testament that foretold the first coming of Christ, there are some 2400 verses throughout the Old and New Testaments revealing God's promises about the return of Jesus Christ (a few listed below). The enormous number of prophetic verses about the Second Coming underlines the vital importance of this event in God's plan for mankind. Consequently, we dare not ignore the prophetic signs pointing to the nearness of His return. God intends to set the Lord Jesus Christ up as King over the earth. There have been many kings to rise and fall throughout history, but God has in mind a PERFECT King for His promised Kingdom.

- Gen 49:10
- Ps 2:1-9
- Isa 11:1-6
- Jer 23:5
- Joel 2:31
- Mal 3:1-2
- Matt 25:1-13
- Luke 1:31-33
- Acts 1:6-7
- Rom 11:25-27
- James 5:7-8
- I John 2:28

The Second Coming - What is it? (2)

The Second Coming is when Jesus Christ will return to earth in fulfillment of His promises and to fulfill the prophecies made about Him. Jesus Himself promised, "At that time the sign of the Son of Man will appear in the sky, and all the nations of the earth will mourn. They will see the Son of Man coming on the clouds of the sky, with power and great glory" (Matt 24:30). Read the proclamation in Rev 19:11-12. Those who witnessed Christ's ascension into heaven after his death and resurrection heard the angels declare in Acts 1:11 that He will return. The Second Coming is the literal return of Jesus Christ to earth as King in power and glory to rule for a thousand years (Revelation 20:1-6).

The OT prophets did not seem to fully understand this distinction between the two comings of Jesus (His birth and His Second Coming) as seen in Isaiah 7:14; 9:6-7; and Zech 14:4. Those who argue that Jesus was not the Messiah because He did not fulfill all the Old Testament prophecies about the Messiah, fail to take into account the Second Coming of Christ, in which He *will* fulfill all the prophecies about the Messiah. Christ's first coming was to stand in our place and receive the penalty exacted for sin. His Second Coming will defeat sin for all eternity.

The second coming should also not be confused with the event referred to as the Rapture. The Rapture refers to a time when Jesus Christ will come to remove all believers from the earth (I Thess 4:13-18; 1 Cor 15:50-54). The church holds many positions on the rapture, but the Second Coming is undisputed.

The Second Coming - Why is it important? (2)

Foremost of all, belief in the Second Coming of Christ is important because it is clearly what the Bible teaches. To doubt the reality of the Second Coming is to doubt the reliability and validity of God's Word. Second, the Second Coming is important because Jesus Himself promised it. If Jesus was wrong about the Second Coming, how can we trust anything else He taught? The Second Coming of Christ is our hope and confidence that God is in control of all things and is faithful to His Word and His promises (Titus 2:13). The Second Coming is also important because it will come at the time when the world is most in need of a righteous King. Rev chaps 6-18 describe the end times prior to the Second Coming of Christ. The world will be devastated, millions of people will perish, and the most evil person in all history will be ruler of the entire world. The Second Coming of Christ puts all this to an end (Rev 19:15-16)

The Second Coming - When is it? (2)
Perhaps no event in the history of the world has been more anticipated than the Second Coming. Every generation of believers, including believers in the New Testament, has strongly believed that Jesus would return in their lifetime (II Thess 2:1-2). Others doubt that it will ever occur (II Peter 3:4). Many have made guesses as to when the Rapture and Second Coming will occur, all incorrect. The Bible declares, "No one knows about that day or hour, not even the angels in heaven, nor the Son, but only the Father"(Matt 24:36). The Bible describes several events which must occur before the Second Coming (Matt 24:4-29; II Thess 2:1-12; Rev 6-18). So, we are to anticipate the Second Coming, but have a biblical understanding of it. We are not to set dates and times, but live our lives as if it could happen any day, any moment (Matt 25:19-21).

Signs of Christ's Return
Matthew 24 and Luke 21 contain Jesus' own words regarding His coming again. Other major references include Daniel 12, II Timothy 3:1-7, and II Peter 3:1-13.

Matthew 24 (The Olivet Discourse)
- V. 1-3--Note the 3 questions Jesus' disciples asked Him. They asked Him when will the Temple be destroyed, what will be the sign of His coming again, and what will be the end of this age. He answered question 1 in Luke 21:20 fulfilled in AD 70. The remainder of Matt 24 and Luke 21 gives His answers to questions 2 and 3.
- V. 4-8--Jesus mentions at least four general signs that will precede His coming......(1) false Christs, (2) wars and rumors of wars—see Joel 3:9-10, (3) unusual disturbances in nature including famines, and (4) earthquakes.
- V. 9-14--Society will deteriorate (lawlessness, rebellion, less love for others, hatred of Christians), false prophets multiply, the gospel will be preached to the whole world   and then the end will come (14)
- V. 15-22--Jesus touches upon the Great Tribulation and refers to Daniel 9:27.
- V. 23-28--Jesus elaborates more on the problem of false Christs and false prophets.
- V. 29-31--Reference again to the Tribulation, also possible reference to the Rapture.
- V. 32-35--Prophecy concerning rebirth of Israel.
- V. 36-39--Jesus emphasizes that no one except the Father knows the time of His return.
- V. 40-44--Another possible reference to the Rapture and the fact that the time of His coming again is unknown. Note His admonitions--Be on the alert, be sure of this, the Son of Man is coming.

Summary of the Signs of the End Times
- Signs of Israel/Jerusalem—Fig Tree blossoming (Israel's rebirth and world political focus).
- Signs of society--plummeting morality, self centeredness, disobedience.
- Signs of the environment—increase in earthquakes, famines, violence, and war.
- Signs of technology—explosion of knowledge, travel, computers, satellites.
- Signs of false teaching (Matt 24:45—cults, apostasy, new age, evil thought to be good.
- Signs of nations—increased centralization of world financial and political power.
- Signs of the gospel reaching the whole world—via television, computers, mission agencies.

Are you ready for the Second Coming of Christ? What are you motivated to do as a result of this study? How is your heart stirred up?

Quotes:
- "We talk of the Second Coming; half the world has never heard of the first." -- Oswald J. Smith
- "We don't have to protect the environment, the Second Coming is at hand"—James Watt
- "Knowing Jesus will return soon makes me want all the more to tell people about him and all that he offers."—Jerry B. Jenkins

Study Topics on God The Spirit

27. Soul and Spirit (1,2)

"What is the difference between the soul and spirit of man?"

The word soul refers not only to the immaterial part of man but the also material part. Unlike man having a "spirit," man is a soul. In its most basic sense, the word soul means "life." However, the Bible moves beyond "life" and into many areas. One of those areas is man's eagerness to sin (story of Adam and Eve, James 1:14-15; Rom 7:17, 21). Man is naturally evil, and his soul is tainted as a result. The life principle is removed at the time of physical death (Gen 35:18; Jer 15:2). The "soul," as with the "spirit," is the center of many spiritual and emotional experiences (Job 30:25; Psalm 43:5; Jer 13:17). Whenever the word soul is used, it can refer to the whole person, alive or after death.

The word spirit refers only to the immaterial facet of man. Mankind has a spirit, but we are not a spirit. However, in Scripture only believers, those who are indwelt by the Holy Spirit, are said to be "spiritually alive" (1 Cor 2:11; Heb 4:12; James 2:26). Unbelievers are "spiritually dead" (Eph 2:1-5; Col 2:13). In Paul's writing the "spirit" was pivotal to the spiritual life of the believer (1 Cor 2:14; 3:1; 15:45; Eph 1:3; 5:19; Col 1:9; 3:16). The spirit is the element in man which gives him the ability to have an intimate relationship with God.

The "soul" and the "spirit" are similar in the manner in which they are used in the spiritual life of the believer. They are different in their reference. The "soul" is man's horizontal view with the world. The "spirit" is man's vertical view with God. It is important to understand that both refer to the immaterial part of man, but only the "spirit" refers to man's walk with God. The "soul" refers to man's walk in the world, both material and immaterial.

"Soul" in Scripture

The usual word for "soul" in the Old Testament (OT) is the Hebrew word nephesh or nepes. This word occurs over 750 times in the OT. (e.g. Gen 2:7). In the New Testament (NT), the Greek word for "soul" is psuche or psyche. This word occurs over 100 times in the NT (e.g. Matt 16:26) In the OT, a human being becomes "a living being" or "soul" only when the "breath of God" is breathed into him (Gen 2:7). The death or disappearance of the "soul" is described as the breath ceasing from an individual (Gen 35:18, Ezek 18:4,20). In modern terms, the "soul" is simply life.

The nephesh is said to be the seat of spiritual as well as physical needs and cravings, including one's need for God's presence (Psalm 42:1; 63:1; 84:2; 119:20). It is the state of consciousness itself. In this connection, nephesh can be used in a general sense to stand for the seat of emotions and experiences (Gen 42:21; Deut 28:65; 1 Sam18:1; Job 30:25; Psalm 6:3; 35:9; 103:1; Jer 13:17). It is associated with will as well as moral and spiritual action (Gen 49:6; Num 15:27). Nephesh can stand for the full range of human needs, desires and feelings, including thought, memory and consciousness (Lam 3:20).

The NT psuche denotes one's inner life or actual personhood. In Matt 10:28 Jesus differentiated between the "soul" and the body. His words indicate that while the body is corrupted at death, the "soul" continues on, though both "soul" and body can end in soul-destroying hell. Souls can also be purified by the truth (1 Peter 1:22). They can be strengthened by ministry (Acts 14:22). Hope in God's covenant promises provides Christians with an "anchor for the soul" (Heb 6:19). In 1 Thess 5:23, Paul's use of "soul," "spirit", and "body" in the same sentence has caused much debate over the meaning and significance of these words. These words differentiate one's personhood, a way of perceiving the totality of human life. Hebrews 4:12, where the word of God is said to penetrate so deeply that it divides "soul and spirit," psuche simply means that the word of God (who is, ultimately, Jesus himself) probes the deepest parts of our personhood, or human self.

"Spirit" in Scripture
The Hebrew word for "spirit in the OT is ruach, appearing over 375 times. It can mean "wind," "breath" or "spirit", but most often refers to the Spirit of God or to the "spirit" of human beings. In the OT, God is seen as the God "of the spirits of all mankind" (Num 27:15). God is the source of "spirit," and that spirit is sovereign to his direction. Death is seen as the release of the spirit God gives (Psalm 146:4). The "spirit" is that which makes possible and sustains life, or the conscious person (Psalm 104:30), but when you take away their ruach, they die and return to the dust (v 29).

God is able to look into the ruach of a person and to examine his or her inner motives (Prov 16:2). The "spirit" of a person is synonymous with the "place" of a person's innermost thoughts. It is there that a person's search for and communion with God occurs (Isa 26:9). Interestingly, both the soul and the spirit are involved in the desire to know God. God can "stir up" the spirit of individuals so that they carry out some undertaking or purpose (I Chron 5:26; Ezra 1:1, 5; Jer 51:1). The "spirit of wisdom" was an extension of the concept of the "spirit" from God which functioned as the animating principle in the prophets. (Num 11:17; Deut 34:9; Isa 28:6).

The equivalent word for ruach in the NT is pneuma, appearing also about 375 times, mostly referring to the Spirit of God, the Holy Spirit. When pneuma refers to the human "spirit" it is that which makes the human being a living person (Luke 8:55). Death results in the release of the "spirit" to God (Matt 27:50; Acts 7:59). The pneuma represents an individual's deepest thoughts and emotions (Mark 2:8; John 11:33; 1 Cor 2:11). The "spirit" – in conjunction with the "body" (soma, 1 Cor 7:34), the flesh (sarx, 2 Cor 7:1) and soul (psuche, 1 Thess 5:23) – represents the whole person.

The pneuma is the realm where relations between God and a human being can take place (Phil 3:3, Rom 1:9; 1 Cor 5:3-5). Coming to faith is seen as a revival of the human "spirit" (Romans 8:10; 1 Peter 4:6). A person's "spirit" can be united with the Spirit of God (1 Cor 6:17) or remain a "spirit of slavery" without it (Romans 8:15). "Spirit" and "flesh" are seen as opposites and contenders within the human psyche. The "spirit" represents the new way of life in communion with God and the "flesh" the old way of sin (Romans 8:1-11). It is the "spirit" that experiences the final salvation, not the "flesh" as such (1 Cor 5:5). While the "flesh" dies, the Spirit of God makes alive (1 Peter 3:18).

The gift of the Spirit marks the beginning of the Christian life and experience (Gal 3:2-5). A person does not belong to Christ unless he or she has the pneuma of God (Rom 8:9); cannot be united with Christ except through the Spirit (1 Cor 6:17); cannot share sonship with Christ apart from sharing in the Spirit (Rom 8:14-17); is not a member of the body of Christ without the Spirit (1 Cor 12:13).

The pneuma from God – from above – is what provides and creates the new birth resulting in spiritual oneness with the Father (John 3:3-8), Jesus and the Holy Spirit (John 14:15-23). Possession of the spirit of God is the defining characteristic of the Christian (Rom 8:9; 1 John 3:24; 4:13).

Quote
➤ "The mind, emotion and will are the organs of the soul (outer man) and cannot worship God. God is known directly through the spirit, the inner man." Watchman Nee, The Spiritual Man

28. Person and Work of the Holy Spirit

There is much confusion and ignorance about the role and work of the Holy Spirit. Most Christians can define to some degree who God is and who Jesus is, but to define who the Holy Spirit is and exactly what He does causes more uncertainty.

Person and Indwelling of the Holy Spirit (John 14:16-17, 14:26, 15:26, 16:8, 16:13-14)

- The third person of the Godhead, the Trinity….a living person….sent by God the Father and God the Son to guide believers into all truth
- He is called the "Helper" who teaches us about the truth and enables us to remember what Jesus said (John 14:26; 16:12-15; I Cor 2:9-16; 1 John 2:27).
- The Holy Spirit lives permanently in every Christian (Rom. 8:9; Gal. 3:2; 4:6; I Cor. 6:19,20) for the purpose of fellowship (Rom. 8:10; II Cor. 13:5) and for the purpose providing spiritual gifts (later lesson), enabling the believer to bear fruit (Gal 5:22-23; John 15:8, Matt 7:16).
- The indwelling of the Holy Spirit must be distinguished from the filling of the Holy Spirit. The indwelling is automatic at salvation while filling is a function of the believer's choice and may be lost through carnality (Eph. 4:30). Filling is commanded (Eph. 5:18) and regained through confession of sin (I John 1:9; Prov. 1:23).

Work of the Holy Spirit

The following verses describe the ministry of the Holy Spirit. Besides each verse(s) summarize what the Holy Spirit does:

- John 14:16-17 _____
- John 14:26 _____
- John 15:26 _____
- John 16:8 _____
- Rom 8:26-27 _____
- I Cor 2:10-16 _____
- I Cor 12:1-11 _____
- Gal 5:22-23 _____
- Eph 1:13-14 _____
- Eph 4:30 _____
- I John 4:1-6 _____

Some other verses that describe other roles/work of the Holy Spirit: Matt. 12:28; Rom. 8:11; I Cor 6:19, II Cor. 3:6; I Pet. 3:18; II Pet 1:21; Rev 22:17

The Sealing Ministry of the Holy Spirit

The sealing work of the Holy Spirit is the basis for our eternal security. The three phases of salvation are given in Eph. 1:13: hearing the truth of the gospel, believing the gospel, then being sealed by the Holy Spirit. A seal is an authentic contract between God and the believer. Seals indicate ownership; God owns the believer, having purchased him from the slave market of sin (Eph. 1:7; 1 Cor. 6:20). The believer is sealed as a guarantee of his eternal security

The Filling of the Holy Spirit

When a person accepts Christ as Savior, the Holy Spirit comes into (indwells) his life permanently. The Holy Spirit indwells for the purpose of glorifying Christ, but indwelling alone does not guarantee that Christ will be glorified by the believer's life. For this reason, Christians are commanded to be habitually "filled" with the Holy Spirit (Eph. 5:18). The verb "be filled" means "to fill up a deficiency; to fully possess; to fully influence; to fill with a certain quality." Here it is in the present passive imperative, so the verb is a command meaning "keep on being filled" with the believer receiving the action of the verb. The filling is by means of the Holy Spirit.

Results of the Filling of the Holy Spirit
- Imitation of Christ: John 16:14; 2 Cor. 3:3; Phil. 1:20
- Perception of the Word: John 14:26; 16:12-14; 1 Cor. 2:9-16
- Witnessing: Acts 1:8; 2 Cor. 3:1-10
- Guidance: Rom. 8:14; Eph. 5:16-18
- Assurance: Rom. 8:14-16; Gal. 4:5,6
- Worship: Phil. 3:3; John 4:24
- Prayer: Eph. 6:18 with Psalm 66:18
- Leadership in Ministry: John 16:13; Acts 10:9,10; Acts 13:2; Acts 16:6

The Holy Spirit Provides Spiritual Power
The book of Acts is the book of spiritual power - where it comes from, how it is obtained, and how it is used. The promise of Jesus Christ to his disciples was "He shall give you another Comforter, that he may abide with you forever, even the Spirit of Truth... He dwells with you and shall be in you." See II Sam 22:40; Isa 28:56, 40:31; 41:10; Dan 11:32; Eph 3:16; I Cor 1:27; II Cor 12:9; 13:4

The Fruit of the Holy Spirit
The fruit of the Holy Spirit is the character of Christ being formed in the Christian who is filled with the Spirit (Gal. 5:22-23) gives the listing of 9 attributes that are the result of the fruit of the Spirit. Love, Joy, and Peace are fruits of mental attitude, Inward thinking that reflects the lack of mental attitude sins and the relaxation which comes from knowing Bible truth. Long-suffering, Gentleness, and Goodness are outward, or directed toward "neighbors." Long-suffering, for example, is a relaxed attitude toward the human race and is a result of having love, joy peace. This is Faith-Rest under pressure which comes from people or Circumstances. Faith, Meekness, and Temperance are fruits directed upward, or God-ward. Humility, for example, is a grace attitude with regard to divine provision that gives glory to God for all support and blessing in life, rather than taking the attitude that one is self-made.

Sins Against the Holy Spirit (1)
The Bible speaks of five types of sin which can be committed against the Holy Spirit.

Sins by Unbelievers Only
1. Resistance of the Holy Spirit: Acts 7:51. This is rejection of Christ and a rejection of the pre-salvation ministry of the Holy Spirit (John 16:7-11) through the sin of unbelief
2. Blasphemy of the Holy Spirit: Matt. 12:31-32. This refers to rejection of Jesus Christ during His ministry on earth (during the previous dispensation, the Age of the Jews).

Sins by Believers
1. Lying to the Holy Spirit: Acts 5:3. Refers to false motivation, approbation lust sin.
2. Grieving the Holy Spirit: Eph. 4:30. Refers to producing sins from the area of weakness in the sin nature. Any sin in the life of the believer which involves a moral or ethical issue.
3. Quenching the Holy Spirit: I Thess. 5:19. Producing human good from the areas of strength in our sin nature, e.g. giving, prayer, witnessing for the purpose of gaining approval. Human good soothes the conscience and keeps the believer from confessing his sin.

Quotes
- "... not by might, nor by power, but by my spirit, says the Lord of hosts." Zech. 4:6
- "Many people have come to Christ as a result of my participation in presenting the Gospel to them. It's all the work of the Holy Spirit."--Billy Graham
- "The work of the Spirit is to impart life, to implant hope, to give liberty, to testify of Christ, to guide us into all truth, to teach us all things, to comfort the believer, and to convict the world of sin"-- DL Moody

Michael J Akers

29. Witnessing / Soul-Winning (1,2)

Jesus said in Acts 1:8 before He ascended that His disciples would receive power when the Holy Spirit would come into them and they would be His witnesses. The term "soul-winning" simply refers to the practice of trying to lead lost sinners to the Lord Jesus Christ for salvation. The Bible praises the soul-winning Christian (Prov 11:30).

The word "witnesses" in Acts 1:8 is the Greek word "martus" where the word "martyr" comes from. A witness (martys) is "one who testifies" (martyreo) by act or word his "testimony" (martyrion) to the truth. This act of testifying is called his "testimony" (martyria). In Christian usage the term means the testimony given by Christian witnesses to Christ and his saving power. Because such testimony often meant arrest and scourging (Matt. 10:18; Mark 13:9), exile (Rev 1:9), or death (Acts 22:20; Rev. 2:13; 17:6) the Greek was transliterated to form the English word "martyr," meaning one who suffers or dies rather than give up his faith. Greek words (15 in number) stemming from "witness" (martys) are used over 200 times in the NT. Acts has 39 instances and the Pauline writings 35.
In Matt 28:19-20 (Great Commission) the translation of the verb "Go" is "As you are going…". Thus, we are to serve as witnesses for Christ continually after becoming Christians ourselves.

Biblical Reasons for Witnessing/Soul Winning
- Isa 43:10-11
- Matt 4:19
- Matt 5:16
- John 15:26-27
- Rom 1:16
- Titus 2:7-9
- Phil 2:14-15
- I Tim 4:12
- I Peter 2:12,15

Biblical Examples of Witnessing
- Jesus in John 4. Note His examples on how to witness
  - He started the conversation very naturally (v 7)
  - He made sure He was alone, no distractions (v 8)
  - He held her interest (v 10)
  - He refused to be side-tracked (v 11, 19, 20)
  - He easily led her into a spiritual discussion (v 13-14)
  - He brought her to face His claims (v 26)
  - He showed the following qualities in a good witness: tact, kindness, answered questions, but always returned to her problem, good listener
- Jesus' other examples
  - To Nicodemus in John 3
  - To the Pharisees in John 8. Note how Jesus responded to the following questions:
    - What you say is not true (v 13); His answer in 14-15a
    - You are boasting (v 13); His answer in 15b-16
    - Where is God? (v 19); His answer in 19
    - Who are you? (v 25); His answer in 25, 28-29; also 8:12
    - How can we become free? (v 33); His answer in 32,34,36
- Philip in Acts 8:25-40
  - Verse 29 empathizes that we are led by the Spirit to witness and He gives us boldness
  - Discuss meaning of Philip's question in v 30

o Note Philip must have been very knowledgeable of the Word (31, 35)
o Other characteristics of a good witness as exemplified by Philip--boldness (30), compassion (27), humility (27), obedience (27), prayerfulness (26), tactful (30,37), enthusiastic (30).
- Peter and John in Acts 4:7-13
- Stephen in Acts 7

How to be Ready to Witness

1. Pray for opportunities—likely explains why some are successful, some are not.(Acts 4:31)
2. Make Jesus central in your testimony (Acts 4:12)
3. Have your testimony prepared in advance (I Peter 3:15)
4. Memorize the four spiritual laws and the pertinent verses, e.g. see http://www.greatcom.org/english/four.htm
5. Be sure all sin is confessed so that you are filled with the Holy Spirit (Billy Graham example)
6. Pray for individual salvation after sharing your faith
7. Suggested questions to ask
   a. What do you believe?
   b. If you died tonight do you know you would go to heaven?
   c. What problems are you dealing with?
   d. What is your understanding of having a personal relationship with God?
   e. May I invite you to receive Jesus as your personal Savior?
   f. If you are not ready, why not?

Hindrances to Effective Witnessing

- Stress and nervousness—It is NEVER easy. Depends on how much you talk about Jesus in your home and elsewhere. Why you need to be in prayer and have the boldness of the Holy Spirit guiding you.
- Lack of preparation
- Fear of rejection, fear of how people will respond (Prov 29:25; John 12:42-43)
- Fear of failure (Matt 9:37)
- Feat of responsibility for a new convert, i.e. having to minister to that person and feeling responsible for his/her Christian walk

Questions

1. Name one or more persons who have had the greatest influence on your Christian attitude/beliefs. What was it about their witness that appealed to you?
2. Name three people to whom you have witnessed. If you cannot name three, then pray about this and be ready to witness.
3. What is your greatest hindrance for being a more effective witness?
4. Who do you know right now to whom you need to talk about their need for salvation in Jesus?

Quotes

➤ "Matt 28:19-20 is the greatest plan by the greatest person concerning the greatest power ever revealed with the greatest promise ever recorded"—Unknown
➤ "If a man goes overseas for any length of time, we would expect him to learn the language of the country to which he is going. More than this is needed, however, if he is really to communicate with the people among whom he is living. He must learn another language – that of the thought forms of the people to whom he speaks. Only so will he have real communication with them and to them. So it is with the Christian Church. Its responsibility is not only to hold to the basic, scriptural principles of the Christian faith, but to communicate these unchanging truths "into" the generation in which it is living." -- Francis Schaeffer

30. Mind and Thoughts

We do not readily think that the Bible says much about our minds and our thought life, but after reading and thinking about the following Scriptures, you will be amazed. A brief comment by each verse is given, what else can the Holy Spirit help you to learn from each passage?

1. Psalm 7:9   _____

2. Prov 7:23   _____

3. Rom 8:5-7   _____

4. Rom 12:1-2   _____

5. II Cor 10:5   _____

6. Col 3:2   _____

7. Phil 2:2-3   _____

8. Phil 4:7-8   _____

9. I Peter 1:13   _____

10. James 1:5-8   _____

The world is filled with temptation and evil desire. And if left unchecked, it will rob and steal one of the most precious things you have—your mind—which is the home and residence of God's holy truth. While many Christians grapple with the issue of how to censor what they (and their children) watch or read, countless others ignore the warnings. Thin excuses abound: "It's just a short program; it won't hurt to watch it.""I know it's wrong, but it's funny and it portrays real life.""I get so tired of all that goodie, goodie Christian stuff. No one can be good all the time."

What we fail to acknowledge is that our minds and hearts are programmed by the material we listen to, read, and watch. It can be truthfully stated "You are what you watch and read." Revisit and mediate on the teachings of Rom 12:2. (1)

The Effects of Sin on the Mind (2)
Our minds operate like huge computers by gathering and taking in data. We may think we forget certain events, names, and faces, but actually until something short-circuits our mental ability, all we experience is sorted and kept. Our ability to retrieve data may seem limited at times. However, each experience, thought, and event remains imprinted on our minds. Only God has the ability to remove those thoughts that are too painful or irrelevant to where we are today in our Christian walk.

When it comes to sin and its effect on our lives, the memory is often difficult to erase. King David helped to establish a pattern of thinking in the life of his family. He regretted his sin with Bath-sheba and did not want it to be incorporated in his son's life. Once Solomon grew to be a man, the temptation to yield to this same sin became very great. God protects us to a certain point. However, when we disobey His will and sin against Him, He allows us to go our own way. He is omniscient, but He will not violate the limited free will He has given you. Therefore, it is illogical to pray to be pure and then pick up a lustful magazine with the expectation that God will stop you.

Once a mind is polluted with sinful thoughts and images, we are easy targets for the enemy's deception. Like pure water, once you put dirt in it, you cannot make it clean again. However, God's truth can help to filter our minds and over time be delivered from a polluted thought life. Hope and deliverance are God's specialty. An intimate knowledge of Him is the key to a healthy thought life. During His life time, Jesus delivered many who were hopelessly bound in spiritual darkness. Just as He opened the eyes of the man born blind, He can remove the darkness from your spiritual vision, but only if this is what you seek. Once your mind grows accustomed to darkened enticement, the only way to renew the light within is through God's Word (read Col 3:2-3). Yielding to sin and temptation simply does not fit who you are in Christ. Now that you are saved, your life has been sealed by the indwelling presence of the Holy Spirit. This is why there is confusion and strife when we become involved in things that go against the principles of God. When we yield to temptation, we open ourselves up to evil and suffer its consequences. Because Christ lives within you, there is a residing desire for purity and identity with God. This is why it feels good to go to church and doing other godly things. The challenge God places before us is to resist the enemy and stand firm in our faith. When we fail to do this we find ourselves drifting along in a sea of guilt and shame. Shame plays an enormous role in defeating Christians. Many find it hard to forget and forgive themselves for what happened in the past. Christ has cleansed you by the shedding of His blood. It is now your responsibility to abide in the safety of His care, because Satan will never grow tired in his assault on your mind. By refusing to think or yield to his temptations, you can drive him from your presence.

Overcoming Impure Thoughts (3)

Our sex-saturated society has led to huge numbers (millions) of men and women of all ages, many of whom are Christians to be plagued and in bondage to the temptations of impure thoughts. Such thoughts are lust and God's Word condemns lust as sin. Lust is purposefully dwelling on sinful, sensual thoughts. These are the wild horses of our mind which must be tracked down, captured, and made obedient to Christ. Impure thoughts lead to many serious problems for the believer:

1. You will come to justify sin. Remember, Satan is the great deceiver.
2. You will live a double life. A public Christian and an evil-doer.
3. Lustful thirst is unquenchable.
4. You will become obsessed. You will be lust's slave, enslaved in bondage of despair.
5. Lust diverts wholesome sexual energy.
6. Thoughts lead to action. Remember Prov 23:7

How to Completely Overcome Impure Thoughts

1. Confess
2. Expose lust's "big lie."
3. Starve the sources.
4. Win with the Word: Ex: Ps 119:9-11, James 1:14-15, II Tim 2:22. Heb 3:1, I Tim 4:12, I Tim 5:2, Col 3:2-7, I Cor 10:13, Gal 5:24-25, Phil 4:7, I Cor 6:18-20, Psalm 19:13-14, Prov 2:12-19
5. Practice "displacement"—must concen-trate your mind on other things (Phil 4:8)
6. Redirect your thoughts.
7. "Drink from your own spring."
8. Turn temptation into spiritual energy. Go immediately to prayer
9. Become accountable. Cannot beat this problem alone
10. Seek deliverance. This sin is usually too powerful to beat by the first 9 steps alone. God will give you deliverance if you work hard at it. As you pursue thought purity, also seek His total deliverance.

Questions

1. From II Cor 10:5 what weapons might Paul be speaking of which can demolish "strongholds" and take "captive thoughts."?
2. Phil 4:7-8: Besides guarding our hearts, what else will the "peace of Christ" guard? What are eight types of thoughts with which we should fill our minds?
3. Col 3:1-2. Where are we to set our hearts and minds? What can a Christian do to develop a heavenly "mindset?"

Quotes

➤ "Even as water carves monuments of stone, so do our thoughts shape our character." –HB Brown
➤ "The state of your life is nothing more than a reflection of your state of mind."--Wayne Dyer
➤ "You are what you think, not what you think you are."—Unknown

31. Conscience

The key to moral excellence (II Peter 1:5) is a strong faith that is strengthened by having a clear, healthy conscience. Conscience is a term that we all think we know what it is or means, but might have a difficult time adequately defining it with eloquent words. A little boy's definition of conscience: "Something that makes you tell your mother before your sister does". Somebody once said the conscience doesn't keep you from doing anything; it just keeps you from enjoying it. Conscience is something that is a three cornered thing in everyone's heart. It stands still when you do good, but if you do bad, the thing turns and the corners hurt the heart a lot. However, if you keep on doing bad, the corners wear off and it doesn't hurt anymore.

The dictionary defines 'conscience' as a moral sense of right and wrong; an inner voice classifying one's thoughts, words and deeds as worthy or unworthy. Like a High Court judge in the domain of human behavior, conscience passes sentence in the court room of the own mind. No one can dethrone conscience without paying a frightening price. One may choose to ignore conscience or momentarily stifle its voice. But those who do this invariably suffer the consequences.

What is conscience biblically?
What does the Bible say about conscience?
  1. Brings conviction—John 8:9
  2. Bears witness—Rom 2:15, Rom 9:1
  3. Persuades—II Cor 5:11
  4. How important a clear conscience is—I Tim 1:5; II Tim 1:3; Acts 24:16, Rom 13:5. Heb 9:14
"Conscience" is found more than 30 times in the New Testament. It literally means "co-knowledge", that is, conscience knows our inner motives and true thoughts. In the Old Testament the Hebrew word for conscience is "leb" usually translated into English as "heart". So when the word "heart" is mentioned in the Old Testament, (e.g. Pharaoh hardened his heart, David prayed, create in me a clean heart; II Chronicles speaking of a tender heart, Psalms using the phrase "upright in heart"), all these references to heart can be speaking to one's conscience.

Seared Conscience (1)
The voice of conscience can be ignored. If we continuously ignore the still small voice of conscience, (the voice of God's Spirit speaking to our souls) we grieve the Holy Spirit: we blunt conscience. The Bible refers to the result as a 'seared conscience.' (I Tim 4:2). It is as though the nerve ends of the soul have become dead and no longer register guilt. This is a deadly condition.

This is an effort to stop the flow of conscience; to silence its voice. Heb 3:13 warns of the danger of being "hardened by the deceitfulness of sin". We see in this day and age a vanishing of community conscience as society becomes more corrupt and more tolerant of worse and worse sin. People are no longer ashamed about their sin; they boast about it. The movies, TV shows, advertising, tabloid publications, the growing acceptance of homosexuality, abortion, the overt greed, especially in athletics, businesses and politics where people lie more than tell the truth--all of these contribute to the defiling of our consciences.

Three ways that the mind sins (2):
  1. Sins of remembering. This is why pornography is so spiritually destructive. Once you implant lurid images in your thoughts, you cannot take them away. While sexual thoughts are prominent, especially among men, other sins of remembering can include past anger, jealousy, harsh words, improper relationships, and other evil deeds.
  2. Sins of scheming. Here is where the mind plots sins of the future like dishonest business dealings, getting back at someone or doing anything that you know is wrong. Prov 6:16-18 tells that one of the abominable sins of the Lord is a heart that devises wicked plans.

3. Sins of imagining. Every imagined sin offends a healthy conscience. We can imagine lust, revenge, hurting someone, winning the lottery, coveting, all kinds of fantasies. The advertising industry thrives on appealing to these kinds of lusts. Are these sins really that bad? Listen to what Jesus said in Matt 15:18-19. James 1:15 warns of evil desires, when conceived, bring forth sin.

Purged Conscience (3)

It is said that: When you fight with your conscience and lose, you win. Indeed when you follow the dictates of your conscience as prompted by Bible truth you can be sure that the Holy Spirit is at work in your life. A guilty conscience is evidence that the Lord's Spirit is at work in your mind. Do not stifle His voice. Instead seek to serve God with a clear conscience. (Acts 23:1, II Tim 1:3)

Good Conscience (Hebrews 9 and 10)

We can have a "good" conscience or a "defiled/wounded/bad" conscience. A good conscience is a conscience cleansed from the defilement of sin, set free to serve God. A good conscience renounces and denies all sin. When we follow a good conscience it commends us, bringing us joy, serenity, self-respect, well-being, and gladness. A person who violates a good conscience will experience shame, anguish, regret, and anxiety.

What can you do to restore a clear conscience? (4)

1. Confess and forsake known sin. The more you read and listen to Scripture, the more your sin will be revealed to you. I John 1 says a lot about confession of sin as an ongoing charac-teristic of the Christian life. The Bible says that we are righteous IF we confess our sins and ask to be cleansed of all unrighteousness, then try to avoid any purposeful sin. In Luke 18:13 Jesus commended the tax collector and condemned the Pharisee. The tax collector saw himself for what he was, a sinner in the sight of God. The truth is--his self-image had never been sounder than at that moment. Rid of pride and pretense, he now saw there was nothing he could ever do to earn God's favor. Instead he pleaded with God for mercy. He went to his house justified, exalted by God because he had humbled himself.
2. Refuse to entertain your old ways of thinking. Everyday, try to re-program your mind (Rom 12:1-2). You will stumble because of long time habits, but remember, confess your sin and refuse once again to give place to evil thoughts.
3. Ask forgiveness and be reconciled to anyone you have wronged. Jesus speaks to this when he says in Matt 5:23-24 to first be reconciled to the person you have wronged before you can adequately and freely worship God and be used by Him.
4. Make restitution; pay back what you have taken.
5. Avoid evil attractions. For example, don't watch or read pornography when you know that this will weaken your conscience and cause you to sin. Job 31:1 made a covenant with his eyes. Or stay away from people you know will have an adverse influence on you. Or don't go to bars and cocktail parties if you have an alcohol problem.
6. Don't procrastinate in clearing your wounded conscience. Guilt feelings can fester into depression, anxiety, other major emotional problems. Deal with the wounded conscience immediately by heart-searching prayer before God.
7. Educate your conscience. To educate our conscience means to subject our conscience to the truth of God and the teaching of Scripture. This will allow our conscience to be more clearly focused and better able to give us reliable feedback. A trustworthy conscience becomes a powerful aid to spiritual growth and stability in our lives.

Quote

➤ "Conscience is probably the number one great argument for the existence of God. It is God's voice to the inner man, our souls." –Billy Graham

32. Spiritual Gifts

Spiritual gifts (or charismata) are gifts that are bestowed on Christians, each having his or her own proper gift (or gifts) to strengthen the church. They are described in the New Testament, primarily I Cor 12, Rom12, and Eph 4. Controversy still exists whether these gifts are as important today as they apparently were in early years of the church. Gifts of speaking in tongues and interpreting tongues are the most controversial. Spiritual gifts were/are part of God's plan for His church, God's "power tools" given to the body of Christ to enable His believers to accomplish works of ministry that otherwise could not be accomplished.

The apostle Paul wrote to the Corinthians, "Now concerning spiritual gifts, brothers, I do not want you to be uninformed" (I Cor 12:1). We ought not to be uninformed about the nature and purpose of spiritual gifts. The first Biblical reference to the term "spiritual gift" is Rom 1:11-12. John Piper teaches that spiritual gifts are for strengthening others. They are not given to be hoarded. To strengthen someone by a spiritual gift means to help their faith not give way as easily when trouble enters their life. We have spiritual gifts in order to help other people keep the faith and maintain an even keel in life's storms. If there is anybody around you whose faith is being threatened in any way at all take stock whether you may have a spiritual gift peculiarly suited to strengthen that person.

Also, spiritual gifts are an expression of faith that aims to strengthen faith. It is activated from faith in us and aims for faith in another. Another way to put it would be this: A spiritual gift is an ability given by the Holy Spirit to express our faith effectively (in word or deed) for the strengthening of someone else's faith.

I Peter 4:10-11 makes four observations about spiritual gifts (1)
1. "Each has received a gift." Gifts are not for a few but for all, and every believer has abilities which the Holy Spirit has given and can use to strengthen others. And it is the supreme joy of life to discover what they are and then pour yourself out to others through these gifts.
2. As emphasized already spiritual gifts are abilities given by the Spirit which express our faith and aim to strengthen the faith of others. They fit together because faith is what the house owner wants in all his stewards and grace is the only currency that can purchase faith.
3. I Peter 4:11 emphasizes that grace can be disbursed through gifts which are word-oriented or deed-oriented. If your gift involves speaking do not rely on your own insight, but look to God to give His words through you. If your gift involves practical deeds of service do not try to do them in your own strength. For then your gift will cease to be a "spiritual gift." It must come from faith and reliance on grace in order to be a "spiritual gift."
4. The aim of all spiritual gifts is "that in everything God might be glorified through Jesus Christ" (v. 11). This means that God's aim in giving us gifts, and in giving us the faith to exercise them, is that his glory might be displayed.

Bill Gothard taught that the Bible describes three kinds of spiritual gifts (2).

1. MOTIVATION:	Romans 12:6-8	Given by God's grace
2. MINISTRY:	I Cor 12:27-31	Given by the local church
3. MANISFESTATION:	I Cor 12:7-11	The result of using our gift

On the other side of this page, the seven motivational gifts from Rom 12:6-8 are described. Each gift has a Biblical personality who exhibited this gift, the main purpose of the gift, 5 or 6 positive (left side) and negative (right side) descriptors of each gift, and how a person having that gift might react to a common life situation, the example being a person who is sick.

PROPHECY (Peter)	Romans 12:9	Proclaim truth, expose sin
-- Need to express yourself		-- sometimes expose others without restoring them
-- Quick impressions of people		-- sometimes jump to conclusions

-- Alert to dishonesty   -- sometimes react harshly to sinners
-- Open about your own faults   -- sometimes condemn yourself
-- Loyalty to truth, not to any one person   -- sometimes cut off people who fail
To a sick person: "What is God trying to say through this illness? Is there some sin you haven't confessed"

SERVING (Timothy)   Romans 12:10   Meets needs, frees others
-- See and meet practical needs   -- sometimes give unrequested help
-- Free others to achieve   -- sometimes let things be too important
-- Disregard for weariness   -- sometimes work beyond physical limits
-- Difficulty saying "no"   -- sometimes neglect God-given priorities
-- Needs approval   -- sometimes resent lack of appreciation
-- Puts extra touches to jobs   -- sometimes frustrated with time limits
To a sick person: "I've brought your mail, fed your dog, watered your plants, washed your dishes"

TEACHING (Luke)   Romans 12:11   Clarify truth, validate information
   Must validate information   -- sometimes becomes proud of knowledge
-- Alert to false teaching   -- sometimes despises lack of credentials
-- Present trugh systematically   sometimes criticizes practical application
-- Gather many facts   -- sometimes shows off research skills
-- Requires thoroughness   -- sometimes rejects faith over substance
-- Clarify misunderstandings   -- sometimes argues over minor points
To a sick person: "I did some research on your illness and I believe I can explain what's happening"

EXHORTING (Paul)   Romans 12:12   Stimulate faith, promote growth
-- Committed to spiritual growth   -- sometimes leaves out family, personal time
-- Able to see root problems   -- sometimes looks to oneself for solutions
-- See opportunities for other Christians   -- sometimes is proud of visible results
-- Raise hopes for solutions   -- sometimes does not finish what is started
-- Turn problems into benefits   -- sometimes treats people as projects
To a sick person: "How can we use what you're learning here to help others in the future?"

GIVING (Matthew)   Romans 12:13   Entrust assets, maximize results
-- Able to see resources   -- sometimes hoards resources for oneself
-- Gives oneself with gift   -- sometimes uses gift to control people
-- Desire to give secretly   -- sometimes rejects public appeals for help
-- Exercises personal frugality   -- sometimes give to projects, not to people
-- Use gift to encourage others to give   -- sometimes cause people to look to giver
To a sick person: "Do you have insurance to cover this kind of illness?"

ORGANIZING (Nehemiah)   Romans 12:14   Plan ahead, complete tasks
-- Able to visualize final results   -- sometimes view people only as resources
-- Need loyalty in associates   -- sometimes builds loyalty with favoritism
-- Ability to delegate   -- sometimes uses delegation to avoid work
-- Alert to details   -- sometimes overlooks faults of people
-- Complete tasks quickly   -- sometimes fails to explain or praise
-- Decisive   -- sometimes forcing decision on others
To a sick person: "Don't worry at all. I've assigned your job to others."

MERCY (John)   Romans 12:15   Remove stress, share burdens
-- Deep loyalty to friends   -- sometimes defends friend to extreme
-- Need for deep friendship   -- sometimes possessive
-- Empathizes with hurting people   -- sometimes tolerates evil
-- Hard to be firm   -- sometimes a poor leader
-- Measure acceptance by closeness   -- sometimes fails to show deference
To a sick person: "I can't begin to tell you how I felt when I learned you were sick. How do you feel now?"

33. Power

A Bible study on power can take many different directions. There is the power of God, power of the Holy Spirit, power of love, power of the Word, power of the cross, power of salvation, power of forgiveness, power of prayer, etc. The word for power in the Old Testament is "pou'-er", indicative of might, strength, force, is used render very many Hebrew terms, the English translation to words like "valor," "rule," "strength," "might," "dominion." The principal words for "power" in the New Testament are "dunamis", and "exousia". The English translation of "exousia" is "authority" (Mark 3:15; 6:7; Eph 1:21) or "right" (Rom 9:21; I Cor 9:6; II Thess 3:9). Power is attributed preeminently to God (I Ch 29:11; Job 26:14; Ps 66:7; 145:11; Rev 7:12). On this attribute of power of God, another word is "omnipotence. The supreme manifestation of the power, as of the wisdom and love of God, is in redemption (I Cor 1:18, 24). The preaching of the gospel is accompanied by the power of the Holy Spirit (I Cor 2:4; I Thess 1:5, etc.). Miracles, as "mighty works," are denoted by the term "powers" (Matt 11:21,23). The end of all time's developments is that God takes to Him His great power and reigns (Rev 11:17) (1).

Power of God (2)

Before Jesus left his apostles and returned to his heavenly home, he told them to wait at Jerusalem until they were given power from God (Acts 1:8). The Bible calls God's power the Holy Spirit. God's power came upon Jesus when he was baptized. Now, Jesus' disciples were to work for him and they would need God's power too! The power of God came down upon them at Pentecost (Acts 2). God's power was upon them because they could speak in different languages. This was necessary so that all to whom they told the story of Jesus could understand, no matter what language they spoke. Peter preached a wonderful sermon. What was Peter's reply to those who questioned what was going on that day?

What kind of power and/or what claim of power is described in the following verses?
- Romans 1:16
- II Tim 1:7
- Matt 6:13
- Mark 5:30
- II Cor 12:9
- Heb 1:3
- Phil 4:13
- Eph 3:14,16
- I Cor 10:13

In reflecting on the claims of these verses, there are two words that should never be part of the Christian's vocabulary: "can't" and "won't". In fact, non-Christians have every reason to use the word "can't" (e.g. "I can't discipline myself') while for Christians, the operative word cannot be "can't", but more often is "won't" (e.g. not "I can't discipline myself", but rather "I won't discipline myself). If there is a "won't" in your life that you've been calling a "can't", pray over this with God using Ps 105:4, Isa 43:18-19, Hab 3:19, and Heb 10:35-39) (3).

Power of the Bible

1. It is powerful to convert unsaved persons. The Word of God is the agency by which faith is generated. (Romans 10:17). It is able to make you wise unto salvation (2 Tim 3:15). It has great and precious promises that through faith you might be made partaker of the divine nature (2 Peter 1:4). The Law of the Lord, that is, the whole Bible, is able to convert you (Psalms 19:7).

2. It is powerful to sanctify believers. (John 17:17-19). Every Christian needs the Bible if he is to grow in his salvation (1 Peter 2:2). Christ uses it to sanctify and cleanse his church (Eph 5:26; Psalms 37:31; 119:11). It is as a fire and like a hammer that breaks the rock in pieces (Jer 23:29).

3. God's Word does not return unto Him void but accomplished the very things for which God has sent it. (Isa 55:11)

Power of Prayer
1. The power of prayer should not be underestimated. (Matt 17:20; II Cor 10:4-5; Jam 5:16- 18)
2. The power of prayer is not the result of the person praying. Rather, the power resides in the God who is being prayed to. I (John 5:14-15). No matter the person praying, the passion behind the prayer, or the purpose of the prayer - God answers prayers that are in agreement with His will. His answers are not always yes, but are always in our best interest. When our desires line up with His will, we will come to understand that in time. When we pray passionately and purposefully, according to God's will, God responds powerfully!
3. God's help through the power of prayer is available for all kinds of requests and issues. (Phil 4:6-7)

Power of the Holy Spirit
1. The main demonstration of the power of the Holy Spirit is how lives are changed through that power (Rom 8:9-11)
2. The Holy Spirit gives believers power to share the gospel with others (Acts 1:8). Think of what the Holy Spirit did with the disciples starting in Acts 2.
3. The Holy Spirit gives us great power to hope (Rom 15:13)
4. Through the spiritual gifts we have power to do things that otherwise we could not do.
5. What power we are given when filled with the Holy Spirit to demonstrate fruit (Gal 5:22-23)

Examples of Christian Power – can you find the Scripture(s) that support these claims?
1. The power to love enemies
2. The power to forgive
3. The power to be content
4. The power to love the unlovable
5. The power to think positive thoughts
6. The power to be patient
7. The power to be merciful
8. The power to be humble
9. The power to be joyful
10. The power to be disciplined and obedient

Question
Think about examples of God's power. Think about the majesty and mystery of the universe. Think about the power to create. Think about the power to overcome death. Think about the power to overcome evil. Think about miracles. Think about how He used Abraham, Joseph, Moses, David, Daniel and Paul and the disciples to accomplish His will against powerful earthly forces. Think about powerful changes that have been made in your life as a result of your faith. Think about the powerful results of prayer that toppled evil regimes throughout history. Perhaps the greatest thought about the power of God is summarized in Luke 1:37 (nothing impossible with God).

Quote
➤ "The power of God is given to enable us to do a spiritual thing in a spiritual way in an unspiritual world." – Malcolm Cronk

Michael J Akers

34. Joy

Joy in the Hebrew (many words) means glee, exceedingly gladness, shouting and singing for joy, cheerfulness and other very positive words. Joy in the Greek ("Chara", sounds like Khar-ah) means cheerfulness, calm delight and exceeding joy. Joy is *true* happiness as human happiness depends on the "happening". Many times in Scripture joy is used in the midst of difficulties we all experience because joy is the foundation for finding peace and contentment even in difficult times. Wayne Blank states that joy is peace of mind that comes from the absolutely certain knowledge that, at the end of it all, glorious eternal life awaits the obedient.

John MacArthur describes joy this way-- We live in a sad world--a world of despair, depression, lack of fulfillment, and dissatisfaction. Man defines happiness as an attitude of satisfaction and delight based upon present circumstances. He relates happiness to happenings and happenstance. It is something that can't be planned or programmed. Biblical joy consists of the deep and abiding confidence that all is well regardless of circumstance and difficulty. It is something very different from worldly happiness. Biblical joy is always related to God and belongs only to those in Christ. It is the permanent possession of every believer--not a whimsical delight that comes and goes as chance offers it opportunity. A good definition of joy is this: it's the flag that flies on the castle of the heart when the King is in residence. Only Christians can know true and lasting joy. A Christian's joy is a gift from God to those who believe the gospel, being produced in them by the Holy Spirit as they receive and obey the Word, being mixed with trials with a hope set on future glory.

Joy in the Scriptures (1)
- Source of Joy—Ps 4:7-8, Ps 16:11
- Reception of Joy—Luke 2:10-11, John 15:11
- Product of Joy--Rom 14:17, Gal 5:22
- Obedience and Joy--Jer 15:16, Luke 24:32, I John 1:4
- Trials and Joy—I Thess 1:8, II Cor 6:10, James 1:2, I Peter 1:6
  - Hope and Joy—Rom 12:12, I Peter 4:13, Jude 24, I Peter 1:8
  - Ever see this verse?—"God makes the dawn and the sunset shout for joy" (Ps 65:8b)
  - Theme of Philippians is the believer's joy.

Elaboration of Joy in the Old Testament (2)
Besides joy in a general sense, as the response of the mind to any pleasurable event or state (I Ki 1:40; Esther 8:17), joy as a religious emotion is very frequently referred to in the Old Testament. Joy is repeatedly shown to be the natural outcome of fellowship with God. "In thy presence is fullness of joy; in thy right hand there are pleasures for evermore" (Ps 16:11; compare 16:8,9). God is at once the source (Ps 4:7; 51:12) and the object (Ps 35:9; Isa 29:19) of religious joy. The phrase "rejoice (be glad) in Yahweh" and similar expressions are of frequent occurrence (e.g. Ps 97:12; 149:2; Isa 61:10; Zec 10:7). Many aspects of the Divine character call forth this emotion:
- His lovingkindness (Ps 21:6,7; 31:7)
- His salvation (Ps 21:1; Isa 25:9; Hab 3:18)
- His laws and statutes (Ps 12; 119)
- His judgments (Ps 48:11)
- His words of comfort in dark days (Jer 15:15,16).
The fundamental fact of the sovereignty of God, of the equity of the Divine government of the world, gives to the pious a joyous sense of security in life (Ps 93:1 f; 96:10; 97:1) which breaks forth into songs of praises in which even inanimate Nature is poetically called upon to join (Ps 96:11-13; 98:4-9). In the case of those who held such views of God, it was natural that the service of God should elicit a joyous spirit (Ps 27:6; I Chron 29:9), a spirit which is abundantly manifest in the jubilant shouting with which

religious festivities were celebrated, and the trumpet-sound which accompanied certain sacrifices (II Sam 6:15; Ps 33:1-3; Num 10:10; II Chron 29:27), and especially in psalms of praise, thanksgiving and adoration (Psalms 47; 81; 100, etc.).

Elaboration of Joy in the New Testament (2)

Emphasis on joy is more prominent in the New Testament. In the four Gospels, especially Luke, joy is conspicuous. It is seen in the canticles of Luke 1 and 2. It is both exemplified in the life and character, and set forth in the teaching of Jesus. In spite of the profound elements of grief and tragedy in His life, His habitual demeanor was joyous, certainly not gloomy or ascetic. Examples:

- His description of Himself as bridegroom (e.g. Matt 9:15, 25:1, John 3:29)
- Defending His disciples for not fasting (Mark 2:18-20)
- The fact that He came "eating and drinking", causing the charge that He was "a gluttonous man and a winebibber" (Mt 11:19)
- His "rejoicing in the Holy Spirit" (Luke 10:21)
- The fact that His presence was found to be congenial at social festivities (Mark 14:3; Luke 14:1; John 12:1) and at the wedding in Cana (John 2:1 ff)
- His mention of "my joy" (John 15:11; 17:13).

The Beatitudes (Matt 5:3-11) describe Jesus' model of His followers having a calm and composed state of felicity (bliss). Furthermore, in Matt 5:12 Jesus describes a more exuberant state of joy of His followers, in sharp contrast to the "sad countenance" of the hypocrites (Matt 6:16). This spirit is reflected in many of the parables. The discovery of the true treasure of life brings joy (Matt 13:44). The three parables in Luke 15 reveal the joy of the Divine heart itself at the repentance of sinners (see especially 15:5-7,9,10,22-24,32). The parable of the Talents lays stress on the "joy of the Lord" which is the reward of faithfulness (Matt 25.21,23). Jesus confers on His followers not only peace (John 14:27; 16:33), but participation in His own fullness of joy (John 15:11; 16:24; 17:13), a joy which is permanent, in contrast to the sorrow which is transient (John 16:22). In the dark days of disappointment that succeeded the crucifixion, the joy of the disciples passed under a cloud, but at the resurrection (Luke 24:41) and still more on the day of Pentecost it emerged into light, and afterward remained a marked characteristic of the early church (Acts 2:46 f; 8:39; 13:52; 15:3).

Paul speaks of joy as one of the fruits of the spirit (Gal 5:22) and of "joy in the Holy Spirit" as an essential mark of the kingdom of God (Rom 14:17). This joy is associated with faith (Phil 1:25), hope (Rom 5:2; 12:12), brotherly fellowship and sympathy (Rom 12:15; II Cor 7:13; Phil 2:1 f). To rejoice in the Lord is enjoined as a Christian duty (Phil 3:1; 4:4; compare 2:17 f; 1 Thess 5:16). In Christ, the Christian "rejoices with joy unspeakable and full of glory" (I Peter 1:8), in spite of his temporary afflictions (I Peter 1:6). Christian joy is no mere gaiety that knows no gloom, but is the result of the triumph of faith over adverse and trying circumstances, which, instead of hindering, actually enhance it (Acts 5:41; Rom 5:3 f; James 1:2,12; 5:11; I Peter 4:13; Matt 5:11,12, Heb 12:2).

Questions

1. Describe an experience where you were joyful, not necessarily happy.
2. What situations in your life produce the greatest joy?
3. What actions can you practice that will produce joy in others' lives?

Quotes

➤ "The best way to cheer yourself is to cheer someone else up"—Mark Twain
➤ "Joy is not the absence of trouble, but the presence of Christ"—William Vander Haven
➤ "The surest mark of a Christian is not faith or even love, but joy"—Samuel Shoemaker

35. Love

Christian love is the very core of our faith. Agape (ah-gah-pay) is the main word used for "love" in the New Testament. There are three principal Greek words which can be translated as "love" in English, each with different connotations. The two most common were *eros*, which refers to sexual love, and *philos*, which means friendship or brotherly love (*eros* does not appear in the New Testament, but *philos* does). Agape love refers to the unearned love God has for humanity — a love so great that God was willing to send his only son to suffer and die on our behalf. So agape love is sacrificial love, love that puts someone else before yourself.

The Bible emphasizes the love of God (John 3:16, I John 4:16), the love of Christ (throughout the gospels) and the absolute important of believers to exemplify love. What are the two greatest commandments? To love God and to love others as ourselves (Matt 22:37-40).

I Corinthians 13
I Corinthians 13 is known as the Love Chapter of the Bible, also called Paul's Hymn of Love. It is said that discussing this chapter is like clumsy hands touching a thing of exquisite beauty and holiness. Although our words will be inadequate we must try to clarify what these matchless words mean to us and to show their meaning in the way that we live our lives. I Cor 13 sets the standards of love (agape) as defined by Jesus Christ. Agage love is Christian love, not human love. In I Cor 13:1-3 Paul states that love is more important than (1) eloquent and excellent speech, (2) prophecy, knowledge, mysteries, and faith, and (3) giving and sacrificing. All of these qualities are worth something only if they are used in love and for love of God and others.

What Love Is and What Love Is Not (I Corinthians 13:4-7)

Love Is	What This Really Means?
1. Patient	Will you suffer for your loved one? Will you overlook others' weaknesses?
2. Kind	Do you speak kind words? Do you do kind things for others?
3. Truthful	Will you confide your weaknesses? Are you honest with others?
4. Sustaining	How well do you handle stress? Are you an example of inner strength?
5. Believing	Do you give the benefit of the doubt? Do you uplift others?
6. Hopeful	Do you remain optimistic? Do you expect the best?
7. Enduring	Do you defend your spouse? Do you defend your employer?
8. Successful	Can you give evidences of this truth? Do you see your relationships growing?

Love Is NOT

1. Jealous	Do you totally trust your spouse? Do you trust your children's decisions? Are you envious of others' success?
2. Proud	Do you submit to your loved ones desires? Do you boast at work?
3. Arrogant	Is there any hidden superiority you feel toward your spouse, children, or co-workers?
4. Rude	How courteous are you? What kind of language do you use?
5. Selfish	Do you truly care for others more than yourself?
6. Touchy	Are you easily irritated? Does your tongue get you into trouble often?
7. Judgmental	Do you hold any grudges? Are you nagging, critical, blameful?
8. Sinful	Any promiscuity in your life? How do you think God sees you as a loving person?

Love Never Fails
I Cor 13:8 makes this simple statement yet it has powerful meaning. Agape love never fails because it embodies loyalty, reverence, selflessness, unconditional acceptance of others faults, weakness, mistakes. Other translations state: Love never dies (Message), Love will last forever (New Living), Love goes on forever (Living), Love never fades out, becomes obsolete, or comes to an end (Amplified).

Love in Everyday Life (1)

The phrase "walk in love" expresses our entire relationship with God and mankind (Matt. 22:37-40, Eph 5:1-2). Those who love God are followers (imitators) of God as His dearly beloved children. Because God loved us, we love Him (1 John. 4:19). Therefore, we imitate Him as dear children.

Now take a moment and think about God. Think about His goodness and mercy toward mankind. Think about His kindness, love, and grace. Think about His love to give Jesus as a sacrifice for our sins. And think about Jesus' love for us to die on the cross. To imitate God is to be like God and to be like God is to love (Matt. 5:43f). God is love (1 John. 4:16). Jesus left an example for us (I Peter 2:2) and Paul commands us to imitate him as he imitates Christ (I Cor. 11:1) whereby we imitate God. And note that we are to love as children. Think about the trusting love a young child has for his parents. John says that we are either children of God or children of the devil (I John. 3:10). Those who are children of the devil are children of wrath (Eph. 2:3) but the children of God are children of light (Eph. 5:8). Jesus is our example of walking in love. He emptied Himself to come to earth in the form of a servant and in the likeness of man was obedient even to the point of death on the cross (Phil. 2:5f). Love is giving one's self as a servant in obedience to God which is an offering and sacrifice to Him. We must be a living sacrifice to God (Rom. 12:1) as we serve Him by faith (Heb. 11:4) in offering the sacrifice of praise to Him, giving thanks to His name, and sharing (Heb. 13:15-16). Therefore the church offers up spiritual sacrifices acceptable to God through Jesus (I Peter. 2:5). We cannot rely on the judgments of men as to what is pleasing to God. We cannot allow ourselves to be deceived by those teaching human doctrines (Eph. 5:6-7; Col. 2) nor may we be partakers with them in evil deeds. We have a grave responsibility to walk in love. A walk in love is not dictated by the doctrines and emotions of men but by God thus imitating Him. Are you walking in love as a beloved child of God? If not, whose child are you?

Other Biblical Teachings About Love
- Lev 19:18
- Deut 4:37, 10:15
- Deut 6:4-5
- Deut 10:12-13
- Josh 22:5
- Isa 43:1-4
- Mark 12:28-31
- Rom 13:8-10
- I Peter 4:8
- Rev 2:4

Questions
1. Joel Hunter once preached that there are six types of unlovable people in our lives--debaters, detachers, demanders, detractors, despisers, and destroyers. Who is an unlovable person in your life to whom you can start showing more agape love?
2. What is really meant by the phrase in I Peter 4:8 "love covers a multitude of sins"?
3. Examine all the statements about love in I Cor 13 and pray over the ones that you know improvement needs to be made in your love life.

Quotes
- "Genuine love is so contrary to human nature that its presence bears witness to an extraordinary power." --John Piper
- "Christian Love, either towards God or towards man, is an affair of the will."-- C.S. Lewis
- "God loves each of us as if there were only one of us."--Augustine
- "The love of wealth makes bitter men; the love of God, better men."--W.L. Hudson
- "Love is like a smile—neither have any value unless given away"—Unknown

36. Sanctification

Sanctification is one of those large spiritual words that intimidate most people and so we tend to ignore teaching and discussion about it. Yet it describes the position and pursuits of a Christian from the time we accept Jesus as our Savior until the time that we die. The Greek word for sanctify is the same word used for holiness or saint ("hagioi") that means 'to separate" or "to set apart". The subject of sanctification and holiness is mentioned over 1000 times in the Scriptures so sanctification is a very important subject, yet few understand it. Here are various descriptions of sanctification:

- The state of separation unto God and our connection with Christ (John 17:16-17; I Cor 1:30; Heb 10:10). Think of this as complete dedication to the Lord.
- The setting apart of believers in Christ for the purpose of fulfilling their calling in this world (John 17:18-19; John 10:36).
- The progressive growth toward the likeness of Christ Himself, a life filled with the fruit of the Holy Spirit (II Thess 2:13; Heb 2:11, 10:14)
- The sovereign act of God to set apart a person for Himself in order that he might accomplish His purpose in the world through that person (Matt 5:48; Rom 6:19-22; examples of Biblical giants like Abraham, Joseph, Moses, David, Daniel, the disciples, Paul).
- Associated with the doctrines of regeneration, justification, and salvation (Eph 2:8-10).

Salvation can be thought of in three phases:
1. Justification—salvation when a person first confesses Christ as Savior and Lord
2. Sanctification—salvation that continues and progresses throughout the rest of the believer's life
3. Glorification—salvation in eternal life when we will be changed into the perfect likeness of Jesus Christ and completely separated from the presence of evil.

Sanctification of Things—set apart for holy purposes
- A day can be sanctified--Gen 2:3.
- A building and its contents can be sanctified—Exo 39:44, Num 7:1
- The house in which a man lives can be sanctified—Lev 27:14
- A mountain can be sanctified—Exo 19:23.

Sanctification of Humans--Discuss these three verses.
- I Thess 5:23
- Heb 12:14—Set apart (1) by God; (2) for God; (3) from sin; (4) unto a holy life.
- II Tim 2:21

There are many Christians who have established very good personal relationships with the Lord, but there still seems to be something missing in their lives. Where is that feeling of well-being? Where is that love, joy and peace of mind? Why is it at times that a believers is no more fulfilled than many nonbelievers are? Could that missing ingredient a believer's life be the sanctification process? This sanctification process is a deeper work in the Lord - and many have not entered into it either because they have never been shown how to properly enter into it, or they really do not want to go this far with the Lord. Once you enter into this sanctification process with the Lord, it can be a bit painful at times, since God will be working with you to expose and prune out all of the negative qualities that He will not want have operating in your personality. This incredible sense of well-being can only be found in the process of allowing God to work His very nature into your own personality, thereby making you to become more holy. A perfect example of this is the 9 fruits of the Holy Spirit. This means that God will start to transmit and impart His love, His peace and His kindness into our personalities. And once this kind of sanctification process starts to occur, this is when you will really be able to start to feel and experience the sense of well-being that God initially created us to have in Him (1).

How are we sanctified? (2)
- By the Word of God—John 17:17. The Word of God reveals sin, it cleanses and purifies us.
- By blood—Heb 13:12
- By chastisement—Heb 12:10-11
- By yielding to God—Rom 6:19
- By ourselves—II Cor 7:1. Daily we must seek out our sin and cast it away, praying for forgiveness and cleansing, praying to live a Christlike life.

Preparatory Sanctification (3)

Preparatory Sanctification is that initial sovereign work of God preliminary to any experience in the life of the person who is to be sanctified (Jer 1:5, I Peter 1:2). Jesus referred to Himself as the One "Whom the Father *sanctified*, and sent into the world" (John 10:36). What He said is that the Father set Him apart and sent Him from Heaven to earth to accomplish the Divine mission of redemption. Therefore, he could say, "And for their sakes I sanctify myself, that they also might be sanctified through the truth" (John 17:19). He had set Himself apart for the purpose for which the Father had set Him apart. In the Father's plan for the Son we see the principle of Preparatory Sanctification.

Positional Sanctification

This is the act of God the Holy Spirit in which He sets apart every saved person. The preparatory work has been going on for some time according to Divine plan, but now that work becomes effective in the life of the individual person. He is now actually set apart as God's possession and for God's purpose (Isa 43:21). We are sanctified by the Blood of Christ (Heb 12:13). All who have received Jesus Christ have been "sanctified by God the Father, and preserved in Jesus Christ" (Jude 1). This is every Christian's position, independent of the length of time one has been saved, how much or how little one knows about the Bible, or how spiritual that person might be. If you have trusted Christ to save you, then you have been set apart once for all; you are God's sanctified one.

Practical Sanctification

Practical Sanctification differs from Positional Sanctification in that Positional Sanctification is solely the will and work of the triune God, while the Practical Sanctification involves human responsibility. Scripture stresses the pursuit of Practical Sanctification (Heb 12:14). It is the will of God for us to do so (I Thess 4:3). Check out these verses that exhort the Christian to seek sanctification:
- I Peter 1:15, 16
- I Peter 2:5.
- II Peter 3:11
- Romans 12:1
- II Cor 7:1
- Titus 2:11, 12

Pursuit of Sanctification

How does one mature in the Christian life? Growth takes time; no short-cut to spiritual maturity.
1. Consider the importance of the Word of God in the Christian's Practical Sanctification—John 17:17, Ps 119:9, 11, John 15:3, Ps 37:31.
2. Know and reckon on the fact that you are dead to sin and self—Rom 6:6.
3. Christians are exhorted to yield their bodies to God—Rom 12:1, I Cor 6:19-20, Rom 6:13.
4. Practical Sanctification involves the surrender of the will—Ps 119:105, Rom 8:14, Eph 5:17.
5. We sanctify ourselves when we walk in the Spirit—Gal 5:16, I Thess 5:15, Eph 4:30.

Quote
- "The work of God's grace by which the believer is separated from sin and becomes dedicated to God's righteousness. Accomplished by the Word of God and the Holy Spirit, sanctification results in holiness, or purification from the guilt and power of sin. Sanctification is instantaneous before God through Christ and progressive before man through obedience to the Holy Spirit and the Word." –Jack Hayford

37. Patience

Patience is the fourth fruit of the Holy Spirit listed in Gal 5:22. Without the Holy Spirit in control of your life, it is practically impossible to be patient. The word for patience in the Bible is "makrothumia", meaning fortitude, longsuffering, a forebearing attitude in provoking circumstances. Patience is enduring or waiting, as a determination of will. It is not merely enduring trials as a matter of necessity. Patience is a strong determination of will, to victoriously overcome the negative things we confront, according to God's will. Being patient, both proaction and reaction, is clear evidence that you are filled and controlled by the Holy Spirit. Yet patience often is very difficult for most believers to practice all the time (1, 2).

Patience of God (1-3)
God's patience delays judgment—Hos 11:8-9; Exo 34:6; book of Jonah; Num 14:18. Our sins deserve God's immediate judgment, but He hears our prayers of repentance and salvation. What a comfort this is to realize is willing wait. God is patient both towards saints and sinners--Neh 9:30; Matt 18:26-34; Rom. 2:4; I Pet. 3:20; II Pet. 3:9, 15.
1. God's patience enables us to endure suffering—James 1:2-4. Paul talks about Jesus' longsuffering in I Tim 1:12-16. God uses our trials to produce patience in us.
2. God's patience establishes hope. Patience is connected with hope, hope of fulfillment and hope of rescue--Rom 5:3-5, 8:19-23; 15:4; Heb 6:12-15; Ps 37:7-9. In fact the Psalms have many verses about patience and hope--25:5, 21; 27:14; 40:1; 62:1; 130:5.
3. God's patience characterizes Christians—Rom 8:18; 13:4. Much of this study focuses on patience as a key demonstration of Christian character.
4. God tells us to put on a heart of patience (Col 3:12).

Some Biblical Examples Of Patience
1. Abraham—Heb 6:15
2. Job—James 3:10-11, 5:11
3. Jesus—Heb 12:2
4. The parable of the persistent widow—Luke 18:8—praying with patience

Benefits of Patience
1. Tolerance for other believers— I Cor 13:4; Eph 4:1-6
2. Requirement for teaching—II Tim 4:2
3. Endure suffering— James 1:2-4, 5:10-11; 1 Peter 2:20; Rom 5:3-4; 12:12; II Thess 1:4
4. Wisdom and power—Prov 14:29, 19:11, 16:32, 25:15; Col 1:11

Patience from James 1:2-4 (word translated as "endurance" is "hupomone" that means patience)
1. What produces patience?
2. What is the result of patience?
3. How does this passage provide a basis for hope in the midst of adversity?
4. Is this passage stating that being patient results in perfection?

How Do We Display Patience?
1. Thank God regardless of our circumstances—Phil 4:4, I Peter 1:6
2. Seek His purposes—ask what can be done while we wait that He desires
3. Stay focused on the ultimate goal—James 4:7-8
4. Thinking before speaking or acting—Prov 15:1-2
5. Remember His promises—Rom 8:28
6. How we treat our family members
7. How we interact with others in a mentoring role.

Negative Consequences of Impatience (4)

- We run the risk of always being dissatisfied, upset, and angry with ourselves for our slow pace of growth and change.
- We easily lose our control and fire off outbursts of anger, temper, and blame on those who are slow to change and grow.
- We become a member of the "throw away" generation, discarding relationships, people, jobs, school, and church whenever things are not working out as quickly as we want them to.
- We waste energy worrying about how slow things are changing instead of directing the energy toward the changes we desire.
- We withdraw prematurely from a helping situation because we are not seeing an immediate pay off for our efforts.
- We sacrifice friendships and relationships prematurely because the other person is not changing as quickly or as thoroughly as we desire.
- We ignore all of the positive gains we and others have made on the road to recovery and growth, only concentrating on what has not yet been accomplished.
- We become pessimistic about life, seeing only the "half-empty cup" rather than the "half-filled cup."
- We will be in such a hurry that we neglect to count our blessings and see how far we have come.
- We lose the ability to take a large goal and break it down into manageable increments.
- We become overwhelmed by the large tasks ahead of us and lose the hope and motivation to keep on trying.

Questions

1. Do you think that patience comes naturally or is it something that is learned as you get older and more mature? Note the progression of Christian maturity in II Peter 1:5-10 and where perseverance fits.
2. What situations test your patience the most?
3. In the Bible, perseverance is often mentioned in the same verse as patience (Matt 24:13; Rom 5:3-4; Gal 6:9; Heb 10:23, 10:36, 12:1; James 1:2-4). Why do these two traits go hand in hand? What is the difference between them?
4. The Bible also frequently mentions a promise along with patience and perseverance (Psalm 37:7-9, 37:34, 40:1-3; Galatians 6:9; Hebrews 6:12, 10:36; James 5:7-8). What are these promises?
5. Read Eccl 7:8 and Prov 14:29.......discuss relationship between patience and pride

Quotes

- "Patience is the quality that makes a man able not simply to suffer things, but to vanquish them"— William Barclay
- "Patience is a virtue, possess it if you can, seldom in a woman, never in a man"—Unknown
- "Patience is the art of hoping"—Unknown
- "Patience is the key to contentment"--Unknown

38. Gentleness and Meekness

Meaning of Gentleness and Meekness in the Bible (1)

Gentleness in the Greek is "praotes", meaning humility, meekness, forgets oneself for the sake of others. "Praotes" is used in the New Testament as
- an attribute of the child of God (Eph 4:1-2; Col 3:12; I Tim 6:11; Titus 3:2)
- an attribute of Jesus Christ (II Cor 10:1)
- the attitude that ought to be displayed when a Christian speaks with and/or needs to correct another (1 Cor 4:21; II Tim 2:25).

In the Old Testament, the word "meek" is not found, but there are several references to the word "humble" or "afflicted" that has the same meaning—Ps 25:9, 76:9, 147:6, 149:4; Isa 29:19.

Meek or meekness is often used today with a negative connotation; it is often used of a person who is perhaps quiet and unassuming or a person who does not stand up for himself. This connotation is not present in the word as used in the Scriptures. Meekness means "appropriately humble, in an evangelical sense; submissive to the divine will; not proud nor self-sufficient nor complains. We may see the reasons behind the choice of the term "gentleness" in many modern versions over the term "meekness," lest any receive the wrong impression about what a Christian ought to be. A Christian is not to be a "pushover," one who does not stand up for what he believes; he is to be gentle, a person who maintains control and grace even under significant duress. The Biblical concept of "gentleness" is a much harder attribute to imbibe than it may originally appear. We may learn about gentleness from the examples of both Jesus and Stephen, for with these two we see first the Jesus whose life we ought to emulate (I Cor 11:1), and Stephen who recognized this need and performed it. Interesting, the only passage in the Gospels where Jesus gave a self-description He called Himself "meek and lowly in heart (Matt 11:29-30). We see that Jesus calls Himself meek (gentle) and lowly in heart (humble), and we see that He best demonstrates this by His death on the cross. We see that Jesus was reviled and mocked in Luke 23:35-37. Stephen also found himself in a similar predicament in Acts 7:54, 57-60

What can we learn from these examples? Jesus and Stephen were certainly gentle in spirit, able to desire the forgiveness for those who were killing them. Would we consider these two "meek" according to the way the term is commonly perceived? By no means! Yet they are certainly meek according to the way the Bible uses the term. Could the same be said of us? Do we attempt to show gentleness even to those who would revile and persecute us? Do we return good for evil, or do we return evil for evil? It is always easier to lose composure and to get angry when we are spoken to or of badly than it is to maintain one's composure and to display the proper attitude of gentleness as seen in the Scriptures. Let us constantly strive to emulate Jesus' gentleness and in so doing further shine as lights for Christ in the world.

Meekness is Love's Humility (2)
1. Meekness is a quiet spirit that is highly valued by the Lord—I Peter 3:4
2. Meekness comes from strength—I Peter 5:5-6
3. Meekness brings blessings—Prov 15:1, 33; James 4:10
4. Meekness obtains grace—James 4:6-7
5. Meekness is teachable—James 1:21
6. Meekness places others first—Phil 2:3
7. Meekness does not criticize—Matt 7:3, Gal 6:1
8. Meekness receives rewards—Psalm 22:26, 25:9, 37:11, 147:6; Matt 5:5
9. Jesus is our example of meekness—Matt 20:28, John 13:14-15, Matt 11:29

Blessed are the meek for they shall inherit the earth (Matt 5:5)

What do you think that the "world" thinks about this? This is one of the best examples of the principle in Isa 55:11 ("My ways are not your ways......."). What the world esteems and values is not what God esteems and values. Worldly people do not like the concept of meekness. The world values what is described in I John 2:16. Believers are not to follow worldly values. We are "not to conform to this world, but be transformed by a renewal of your mind......" (Rom 12:2). We are to be gentle and meek.

Questions (Some discussion follows, but try to answer these without reading the discussion)
1. What does meekness look like?
2. How can you defend the position that meekness is not weakness?
3. What does Jesus mean by "they (the meek) shall inherit the earth"?

What does meekness look like?

Think of examples in your own life......family members, neighbors, co-workers, Christian brothers and sisters who you believe have exemplified the character of meekness. Here are some basic examples:
- Someone who has no arrogance in their character
- Someone who has a servant's heart
- Someone who is strong, yet has a teachable spirit ("strong, silent type")
- Someone who is even-tempered, who can show displeasure without insulting others
- Someone who does not pity himself/herself
- Someone who is always grateful for what they have
- Someone who is quite confident that God is always with him/her
- Someone who has peace of heart and mind

What are other examples?

How can you defend the position that meekness is not weakness?

From a worldly view, meekness is not something anyone would desire to have, especially if one is ambitious about success in the businessworld, "making it to the top", and being respected by others. The world teaches that success requires assertiveness, being tough, and doing whatever you have to do to succeed. Is a person like this truly "attractive" and truly earns others' long term respect? Yet Jesus said that "blessed are the meek". In the descriptions above, do these portray someone who is truly weak or someone who knows who they are, where they are going, and has nothing to prove? Do not these descriptions portray someone who is extremely strong? Can anyone who thinks more deeply about the meaning of meekness conclude that the meek are "doormats"? Also the promise of Jesus' statement here is that the meek shall be blessed (happy, contented). Is the assertive/aggressive person happy and full of contentment? Lastly, think of your image, based on the gospels, of Jesus' personality. Does He come across as a weak person in all that He faced and did? Jesus depended on God for His strength and wisdom while on earth and the meek person can do the same. Having the strength and wisdom of God on your side is not a position of weakness

What does Jesus mean by "they (the meek) shall inherit the earth"?

Jesus likely was thinking of Ps 37:11, perhaps also Ps 25:12-13 and 37:9, 22. Inheriting the earth could mean receiving all of God's promises just like His promise to Abraham (Gen 15:7). It could mean receiving all God's blessings in life (Prov 3:9-10; Mark 10:29-30). And it could be referring to the new heaven and new earth (II Peter 3:13; Rev 21:1).

Quotes
➤ "Glances of true beauty can be seen in the faces of those who live in true meekness."--Thoreau
➤ "The true gentleman is God's servant, the world's master, and his own man"—Unknown

39. Self-Control

Self-control is the last attribute listed in Gal 5:22-23 of the 9 fruits of the Holy Spirit. Keep in mind that while there are 9 attributes of the fruit of the Holy Spirit, and some call these individual fruits, the verb tense is singular----"The fruit of the Holy Spirit is......". Therefore, a spirit-filled, spirit-led person will have all of these attributes of the fruit of the Spirit, not just some but not others.

The definition of self-control is readily understood, yet the practice of self-control is a daily, difficult challenge for many people, even Christians. Self-control in the Greek is "egkrateia" (eng-krat-i-ah) that means temperance, self-control in appetite, moderation in all things, the final mark of perfection. If a person claims to be a Christian yet cannot control certain aspects of his/her life, this claim is empty. Other verses that use the same Greek word are Acts 24:16 and II Peter 1:6

Negative Desires That Must Be Self-Controlled
- Sexual immorality—I Cor 6:18 (Greek word for immorality is "porneia" that includes adultery, incest, harlotry, and fornication) I Cor 7:5, 9; I Thess 4:3
- Appetite (not just food)--Deut 21:20; Prov 23:2; II Cor 10:5; II Tim 3:1-9; II Peter 1:5-7
- Greed/Self-indulgence—Matt 23:25
- Temper/Anger—Eccl 7:7-9; Matt 5:22-24 (note 3 "whosoever's" in v. 22); James 1:19
- Laziness/Unwillingness to be disciplined—James 1:6-8
- Any desire to sin—all addictions—Prov 25:28; Rom 13:14; II Tim 3:1-5; Titus 2:11-14

Positive Desires That Should Be Self-Controlled
- Obedience—e.g. use of the talents God has given us—I Cor 9:24-27
- Submission—Rom 12:1
- Exercise/Taking care of our bodies—I Tim 4:8; I Cor 6:19-20; I Thess 4:4
- Priorities—Matt 6:33
- Time—Eph 5:15-19

How To Have Self-Control (I John 2:16)
- Controlling our eyes—Job 31:1; Prov 6:17; Matt 6:22; 18:9,
- Controlling our minds— Prov 16:9; Rom 8:7; Phil 4:8; II Tim 1:6-7
- Controlling our mouths—Eph 4:29; Col 3:8; James 1:19, 3:2, 3:9-10
- Controlling all our weaknesses—II Cor 12:8-9

Three Principles for Developing Self-Control (1)
1. Satisfaction comes from self-control, not self-indulgence. Read Prov 25:28. In the ancient world, a city that had no walls, especially a city that previously had walls and whose walls were broken down, was a city disgraced. It was vulnerable and it was humiliated. A lack of self-control does bring shame, it does bring humiliation. For an example, go back to the book of Judges and read about Samson–the Old Testament's poster child for self indulgence. Look at the way his lack of self-control leads him into sin, disgrace, and humiliation. We think that giving in to our desires will satisfy us, but very often the reverse is true. When I am out of control is when I am miserable. It is when I am under control that I am satisfied and at peace. One old writer wrote these words about this fruit of the Holy Spirit, "Happiness is to be found rather in checking our inclinations than in gratifying them.... The more we indulge them, the more we increase them.... Self-denial has its pains as well as pleasures, but it has less pain and more pleasure than indulged appetite."

2. Self-control that is the fruit of the Spirit is really Christ-control. But that is not enough by itself to produce the fruit of the Spirit. After all, a businessman who denies himself the pleasures of friends

and family in his pursuit of wealth and success is not exhibiting the fruit of the Spirit. Nor is the Christian who checks certain impulses because indulging them would not be acceptable in one's circle of Christian friends. There is a problem here even in the way this word is translated. The idea of self-control almost seems paradoxical in a list of fruit of the Spirit! Where does the self come in here in the fruit of the Spirit? Well the 'self' component in this expression is in the English, but it is not actually in the Greek. The Greek word simply refers to mastering one's desires and one's actions. This is not about control for myself or by myself–ultimately this is about control by and for Christ. The self control that is the fruit of the Spirit means that we say no to ourselves so that we say yes to the Christ. Read Titus 2:11-14. We deny ourselves, we control ourselves, because we love Christ and we want to please Him. We master our desires in order to worship Him. Food is His gift; we eat in moderation with thankfulness to gain strength to serve Him. Rest is His gift; we rest, not in idle self-indulgence, but so that we may be refreshed to serve Him. Sex is His gift; we use it to serve Him in becoming one with our spouses in marriage and in practicing chastity outside of marriage. We master our desires, our time, our thoughts, indulgences for nice things––all in order that we might offer all we are and all we have to Him as acts of worship. The self-control that is the fruit of the Spirit is not control by or for me. The fruit of the Spirit is submitting our desires and our opportunities to Christ.

3. We must understand that self-control requires practice. Self-control is not like one of those ads you see on television late at night promising a whole new you in six weeks. The fruit of the Spirit does not grow that way. The Spirit has to produce this in us, but none of the fruit of the Spirit grows without our engagement. It is not that you pray for it one night and get up in the morning and, poof, you have it all in full measure. Self-control in particular requires practice because self-control is a skill. It may take years to learn self-control in some areas of your life or mine. It may not always be evident when you are making progress. At times it may seem easier or harder; at times there may be areas where you thought you had it and all of a sudden it breaks out and it seems to be a struggle again. That is why we need grace in our pursuit of self-control. It is a long-term process that we pursue by faith in God's promise that He is at work in us. We pursue self-control as part of the life-long task of expressing in our daily lives the new life that Christ has given us by His Spirit. We live in gratitude for His grace and His mercy that covers all our self-indulgence and all of our sin. All the while, we can be secure in the promise of Phil 1:6, that God is always at work in us, enabling us to keep making progress in our journey toward Christian maturity.

Questions
1. What areas of your life do you know deep in your heart are not controlled by Jesus Christ?
2. What are examples of self-control that you see in your life? In others' lives?
3. Is self-control the same as self-denial? In light of some of the points made in this study, what does self-control really mean with respect to the role of the Holy Spirit?
4. Why do you think that self-control was the last of nine fruits of the Holy Spirit? Does this give it any greater prominence than the other fruits and/or is it a culmination of all the fruits

Quotes
➢ "When wealth is lost, nothing is lost; when health is lost, something is lost; when character is lost, all is lost."--Billy Graham
➢ "Any fool can criticize, condemn, and complain but it takes character and self control to be understanding and forgiving."—Dale Carnegie
➢ "Hold tight rein over three Ts—thought, temper, and tongue—and you will have few regrets"—Teen Esteem
➢ "Choose rather to punish your appetites than be punished by them"—Magnus Maximum

Study Topics on God's Believers

40. Fellowship and the Church

Definition and Purpose of Church.

The Greek word for church is "ekklesia", meaning "an assembly of called out ones". Jesus first used the word in Matt 16:18. Note the significant promise in this verse. The word church does not mean a physical facility, a denomination, even any kind of organization. The church is people, a group of people who are together to worship Jesus Christ, learn and obey His Word, and to stimulate and encourage one another. Here's how the Bible defines the church:

- The body of Christ—Rom 12:4-5, 16:16; I Cor 12:12-27; Eph 1:22-23; Col 1:18
- The bride of Christ—Eph 5:23-25-27, 32; Rev 21
- The family of God—Eph 3:14; Heb 2:11
- The house, household, or building of God—Eph 2:19:21; I Tim 3:15; Heb 3:6
- The flock of God—Acts 20:28; I Peter 5:2-3
- Other verses where "church" is stated: Acts 11:26

There are two broad types of church—the universal church and the local church. The universal church is all Christians on earth including all dead Christians (Matt 16:18; Heb 11:12-13, refer to verses above). The local church obviously is any gathering of Christians in a single location. You only need two or three together to have a local church (Matt 18:19). Local churches are mentioned in several of Paul's letters, e.g. Rom 16:1; I Cor 16:1; II Cor 8:1.

Christians are commanded to be part of a local church. Many Christians believe that they can practice their faith and worship God without being part of a church. Reasons for not attending church include pride, rejection, and rebellion. This violates such Scriptures as Acts 2:42-47; I Cor 14:26; Heb 10:24-25. Discuss.

Acts 2:42-47 defines the purpose of the church

- To praise, worship and obey Christ
- To learn God's Word and how to apply it
- To pray together, and celebrate the Lord's supper together
- To foster fellowship and develop communities of hope, healing, and life.
- To bring people to a living faith in Christ

Some churches are failing or dysfunctional. Why? Some answers include failure to preach and emphasize God's Word, hypocrisy, scandal, lack of love amongst members (e.g. I Cor 11:18). What else can cause a local church to become dysfunctional? Read I Cor 11:22…..what might Paul be referring to by "Or do you despise the church of God…?

Fellowship

Life is meant to be shared. God intends for us to experience life together. The word fellowship is translated from the Greek word "koinonia". This word means an association, community, or communion. To be involved in Christian fellowship with others means to share your life with others. We share our lives with others and also with Christ who promises to be with us when even two or three are gathered together in His name (Matt 18:20). Fellowship with Christ and other believers involves feeding on the Word together. Sometimes it means eating meals together (Acts 2:46). In fellowship we share our time, our gifts and talents, both spiritual and natural. We also share of our money as God leads, and according to the needs (II Cor 9). Christian fellowship exists not only to meet the needs of Christians - emotionally, socially, mentally, spiritually and where necessary, financially. It also exists to demonstrate to the world the meaning of Christian love and to call people out of the world into that fellowship with Christ and His body. In fellowship with Christ and with one another, we are coming not only to receive but also to give.

Real fellowship is more than just showing up. It is experiencing life together. It includes all the "one anothers" found in the Bible.

- Love—John 13:34-35
- Depend on—Rom 12:5
- Be devoted to—Rom 12:10
- Show honor to—Rom 12:10
- Rejoice with—Rom 12:15
- Weep with—Rom 12:15
- Same mind toward—Rom 12:16
- Do not judge—Rom 14:13
- Accept—Rom 15:7
- Counsel—Rom 15:14
- Greet—Rom 16:16
- Wait for—I Cor 11:33
- Care for—I Cor 12:25
- Serve—Gal 5:13
- Bear burdens—Gal 6:2
- Be kind—Eph 4:32
- Forgive—Eph 4:32
- Forbear—Col 3:13
- Encourage—I Thess 5:11
- Build up—I Thess 5:11
- Stir up—Heb 10:24
- Be hospitable—I Peter 4:9
- Minister gifts to—I Peter 4:10
- Be humble to—I Peter 5:5
- Do not speak evil—Jam 4:11
- Do not grumble against—James 5:9
- Confess faults—James 5:16
- Pray for—James 5:16
- Fellowship with—I John 1:7

Why is fellowship so important?

1. God desires His people to be in relationships—Gen 2:18; Matt 18:20; John 13:35; Col 3:18-21.
2. We are influenced by who we interact with the most—Prov 13:20; I Cor 13:20
3. Every Christian has a responsibility to practice the "one anothers" (see above) and especially to encourage others—I Thess 5:11; Heb 10:24-25.
4. Heb 10:24 is a commandment from God that we must not forsake assembling with others.
5. God desires us to serve one another; we cannot do this without fellowship—Eph 4:13

What is the difference between real and fake fellowship? (1)

1. People experience authenticity. Genuine, heart to heart sharing. People being honest about whom they are and what is happening in their lives. Fake fellowship involves pretending, role playing, politicking, superficial politeness, shallow conversation. Discuss James 5:16. We only grow by taking risks and the most difficult risk of all is to be honest with ourselves and with others.
2. People experience mutuality. This is the art of giving and receiving. Discuss Romans 1:12. Mutuality is the heart of fellowhip: building reciprocal relationships, sharing responsibilities, and helping each other.
3. People experience sympathy. Sympathy meets two fundamental human needs—the need to be understood and the need to have your feelings validated. Every time that you understand and affirm someone's feelings, you build fellowship. Discuss Gal 6:2 and Col 3:12.
4. People experience mercy. Fellowship is a place of grace, where mistakes aren't rubbed in but rubbed out. You cannot have fellowship without forgiveness. Discuss Col 3:13.

Questions

1. How do we connect to one another at a more genuine, heart-to-heart level?
2. Why do so many people resist fellowship?
3. Are relationships a high priority with you?
4. Does your level of involvement in your church show that you love and are committed to God's family?

Quotes

➤ "The greatest gift you can give someone is your time. The essence of love is not what we think or do or provide for others, but how much we give of ourselves. Men, in particular, often don't understand this." --Rick Warren, p. 127 of Purpose Driven Life
➤ "Church isn't where you meet, it isn't a building. Church is what you do. Church is who you are. Church is the human outworking of the person of Jesus Christ. Let's not go to Church, let's be the Church."—Bridge Willard
➤ "Our love to God is measured by our everyday fellowship with others and the love it displays."—Murray

41. Christian Calling and Service

Calling (1)

Before a person is saved in Christ, he/she is called by God (John 6:44). While there are many examples in the Bible of God calling people to carry out a mission (e.g. Noah, Abraham, Moses, the disciples, Paul, etc), most of God's calling is not direct other than the written or spoken gospel message (Rom 10:13-17).

In Matthew 22:14, Jesus said "For many are called, but few are chosen". Being called is being invited by God to repent of our life without Him and enter into a new life with Him. He wants a relationship with His people and He calls us through His Word. People must recognize a need for change in their lives and that recognition comes through His Word. Without His Word we would never recognize a need for change.

However, besides recognizing a need for change, people must also respond to that need and repent of their sin. By both recognizing and responding to God's call, people are chosen for a relationship with God. According to Jesus in Matt 22:14, many are called (recognized their need for Christ), but few are chosen (respond to the need for repentance and relationship).

But recognizing a need for change is only recognizing God's calling. Only those who respond and repent are *chosen* for a special relationship with Him in the spiritual Body that is His Church. Paul addresses those who have accepted God's invitation as "the church of God . . . , those who are sanctified in Christ Jesus, *called* [invited] to be saints, with all who in every place call on the name of Jesus Christ our Lord" (1 Cor 1:2). Those who repent and are baptized (Acts 2:38) are then chosen "for salvation through sanctification by the Spirit and belief in the truth" (II Thess 2:13). God invites many more into this special relationship than respond. However, the Bible reveals that most people who are called do not respond to their invitation for several reasons. That is why many more are called than are chosen for salvation today. The parable of the sower (Matt 13:18-23) is a great example of the difference between calling and chosen. Only one of four types of soils bears fruit. Bearing fruit is evidence of a person having a close personal relationship with God the Father through Jesus Christ our Lord.

God's Callings (2)

1. Called of Jesus Christ to separation, obedience and ministry—Rom 1:1-7; I Cor 1:1-2; Jude 1:2
2. Called to fellowship with Jesus—I Cor 1:4-9
3. Called to walk a narrow way with Him—Matt 7:13-15; Luke 13:23-28
4. Called to obey Him—Luke 6:46-49
5. Called to see Him as the source of our wisdom and power—I Cor 1:23-24
6. Called to share His victory over the spiritual forces of evil—Rev 17:12-14
7. Called to share His holiness and glory—Rom 8:28-30
8. But few respond to His call with true faith-Matt 20:12, 22:14; Luke 8:11-15; II Tim 1:13-15; 18, II Tim 2:3-5; Matt 25:1-13.

Seven sovereign calls of God (3)

1. Call to salvation (Rom 8:28-30)
2. Call to sanctification (I Thess 4:3, 5:23-24)
3. Call to service (John 15:16; I Cor 1:26-28; Eph 2:10)
4. Call to separation (II Cor 6:14-18)
5. Call to sonship (I John 3:1)
6. Call to subjection (Eph 6:1; Eph 5:22; I Peter 2:18; I Peter 2:13-14; Romans 12:1-2)
7. Call to suffering (I Peter 2:21; John 16:33; Phil 1:29)

Ostwald Chambers (Sept 13, My Utmost for His Highest)

The greatest crisis we ever face is the surrender of our will. Yet God never forces a person's will into surrender, and He never begs. He patiently waits until that person willingly yields to Him. And once that battle has been fought, it never needs to be fought again.

- **Surrender for Deliverance.** "Come to Me . . . and I will give you rest" (Matt 11:28). It is only after we have begun to experience what salvation really means that we surrender our will to Jesus for rest. Whatever is causing us a sense of uncertainty is actually a call to our will— "Come to Me." And it is a voluntary coming.

- **Surrender for Devotion.** "If anyone desires to come after Me, let him deny himself . . ." (Matt 16:24). The surrender here is of my SELF to Jesus, with His rest at the heart of my being. He says, "If you want to be My disciple, you must give up your right to yourself to Me." And once this is done, the remainder of your life will exhibit nothing but the evidence of this surrender, and you never need to be concerned again with what the future may hold for you. Whatever your circumstances may be, Jesus is totally sufficient (see II Cor 12:9 and (Phil 4:19).
- **Surrender for Death.** ". . . another will gird you . . ." (John 21:18 ; also see John 21:19). Have you learned what it means to be girded for death? Beware of some surrender that you make to God in an ecstatic moment in your life, because you are apt to take it back again. True surrender is a matter of being "united together [with Jesus] in the likeness of His death" (Rom 6:5) until nothing ever appeals to you that did not appeal to Him. And after you surrender— then what? Your entire life should be characterized by an eagerness to maintain unbroken fellowship and oneness with God.

Service

All Christians are called to serve one another. Review the "one anothers" given in the study on Fellowship and the Church. Our model is Jesus Christ who said in Mark 10:45 that He had not come to be served but to serve, even to the point of sacrificing His life for the rest of us. Eph 4:12-13 gives the reasons why Christians are given spiritual gifts

A Servant of God (4)

- Does not live to please yourself, but to please only God (Rom 15:1-3; Phil 2:7-8; Matt 20:26-28).
- Serves others in need (Matt 19:21; Col 3:17; I John 3:17-18; Luke 6:36; Eph 5:1).
- Does not serve the flesh (Rom 6:4-13), but lives to the Spirit daily and thus puts the evil desires of the flesh to death (Gal 5:16, 19-21; I Peter 3:18; Rom 8:12-14).
- Visits people in hospitals, always ready to help those who are needy with food, lodging, etc (Eph 4:28, Matt 25:33-40)
- Is a humble attitude when serving these people, as Abraham and Lot did (Gen 17:3; 18:2)
- Lifts people's spirits with his words of love, hope and joy (Heb 10:24; I Thess 5:11; Eph 4:29).
- Does all good works in the name of Jesus Christ, commanded to do by Christ (Col. 3:17).
- Keeps God's word by practicing righteousness (I John 3:7; 2:29). This is how he practices his faith, and it works because it is a faith of works (James 2:14-26). The person who does not practice righteousness daily is not a servant of God (Rom. 10:5-6, 10; I John 3:10).

Questions
1. How were you called? Are you a servant of God as defined by God's word?
2. Why do people reject God's calling? (Matt 7:13-14; Acts 13:46; I Peter 4:17)
3. Is it ever permissible to be selfish? Why or why not? Examples?
4. Is it possible to serve without loving? Is it possible to love without serving?

Quotes
- "God doesn't call us to be successful. He calls us to be faithful."--Unknown
- "The place God calls you to is the place where your deep gladness and the world's deep hunger meet"—F. Buechner
- "Be ashamed to die until you have done something for humanity"—Douglas MacArthur

42. Tests and Temptations

A previous study (#24) focused on suffering and persecution with the perspective of that study being the experience of actual suffering and how Christians can deal with it. This study focuses more on the struggles Christians face in dealing with the temptations to do wrong and the testing of our faith during times of temptation. The word for temptation in the Greek is "periasmos" that means "a putting to proof by the experience of evil". God allows temptation (James 1:12-13) although it is not He who tempts us (James 1:13). Everyone is tempted, even Jesus (Matt 4, Heb 2:18, 4:15). Being tempted is not wrong, but how we respond to temptation can be wrong, i.e. when we given in to temptation (e.g.: Adam and Eve in Gen 3; Samson in Judges 15; David in II Sam 11:2-5). Life's tests and temptations are temporary but rewards for withstanding and defeating them are eternal.

How Satan Attacks Christians?
It is not God, but Satan who tempts us. It was Satan, not God, who tempted Adam and Eve. It was Satan who tempted Jesus Christ. The late Adrian Rogers once preached on Satan's "LSD" from James 1:12:18 and established the following table that describes the sources and defeat of temptation in our lives.

Source of Temptation	Seat of Temptation	Season of Temptation.	Subduing Temptation
Flesh (Internal/Physical foe)	Body	Younger age	Flee (I Cor 6:18)
World (External/Emotional foe)	Soul	Middle age	Faith (I John 5:4)
Devil (Infernal/Spiritual foe)	Spirit	Old age	Fight (James 4:7)

Specifics of satanic temptations---what he attacks and examples:
1. Our minds—various philosophies (e.g. humanism); vain deceit; daydreaming (uncontrolled mental thoughts); doubting the Bible; intellectual pride (pastors); obsessions, grudges; doubts, worry, anxiety; inferiority attitudes; overall discouragement (old age, criticism from others).
2. Our realm of experiences--bad experiences; life's pressures, being too busy, annoyances; sleeplessness; laziness; living too much in our past; cursing; tragedies; feelings ("I don't 'feel' like I'm saved anymore because of what I have done or not done"). Plays on our moods Confusion among physical, spiritual, psychological realms--physical illness is not spiritual or psychological, but Satan will try to convince us that it is; sin is not psychological such that we can explain it away, eg homosexuality. Sin is a spiritual problem; personalities related to "spirituality"......wrong!
3. Our assurances (certainties become uncertainties)--We are not really saved; our faith is shaken; guilt of past not forgiven; God is not always present; the Holy Spirit leaves us

Resisting Temptation
Temptation is won or lost at the spiritual level (Eph 6:12-13). God desires that we endure when we are tempted and promises that He will provide a way out (I Cor 10:13). Temptation always involves choice - do we obey God or give in to our own desires? Yet we all know that overcoming the potential addictive power of temptation is never simple.
1. We resist temptation through God's Word as Jesus did in Matt 4. Jesus was tempted by the lust of the flesh, the lust of the eyes, and the boastful pride of life, the three primary temptations of the world are given in I John 2:15-16
   a. Lust of the flesh—Satan tempted Jesus to break his fasting (Matt 4:3-4).
   b. Lust of the eyes—Satan tempted Jesus by showing Him all the kingdoms of the world and told Him they were His if He would worship him (Matt 4:8-10)
   c. Boastful pride of life—Satan tempted Jesus, just like he tempted Adam and Eve, by trying the twist what God had said and trying to appeal to the pride of man (Matt 4:5-7).
   In each of these satanic temptations Jesus quoted Scripture to overcome the power of Satan and keep him from being successful in defeating our Lord.
2. We resist temptation by employing spiritual weapons of warfare—II Cor 10:3-5. Note the importance

of controlling our thought life.

3. We resist temptation through the armor of God—Eph 6:10-17. D. Martyn Lloyd-Jones wrote a 373 page book (The Christian Warfare, Baker, 1976) based on 4 of these verses (Eph 6:10-13). Note that the armor of God that resists satanic attacks (schemes of the devil—Eph 6:11 and I Peter 5:8) include 5 defensive weapons (truth, righteousness, gospel of peace, faith, and salvation) and one offensive weapon (sword of the Spirit/the word of God).

4. Learn and memorize Bible verses that can/will help in times of temptation. Examples include Rom 8:2, I Cor 15:57, and those listed in the "LSD" table.

The Bible contains many examples of those who failed to resist temptation and those who were successful in resisting/overcoming temptation

Failures	Overcomers
Adam and Eve—Gen 3	Abraham—Gen 14:22-24
King David—II Sam 11 (although David later was convicted of his sin and repented)	Elisha—II Kings 5:16
Samson—Judges 16	Peter—Acts 8:20
Achan—Joshua 7	Jesus—Matt 4 and Luke 4:5-8

How can you have victory over temptation? Temptation is a fact of life for the Christian and perhaps the most difficult challenges we face in our lives. However, take comfort in knowing that the Bible says that we already have victory in Christ Jesus (I John 4:4; I Cor 15:57, many other references)

James 1:12-16

This is an excellent passage to study and discuss many questions about testing and temptation:.
1. What two arguments does James use to demonstrate that God is not the source of temptation
2. What is the ultimate source of temptation?
3. Why is temptation so dangerous
4. What are we not to be deceived about?
5. God does not tempt us, but He will test our faith. What is the difference?
6. Why doesn't God protect His people from temptations?
7. What are some specific activities in your life that lead you to temptation?
8. What do you read, watch, listen to, who do you envy, what childhood experiences have affected your bad habits today?
9. Can anyone eradicate temptation totally?

Twelve Biblical Purposes for Testing and Tribulation (1)
1. To become stronger Christians (James 1:3-4)
2. To bring honor to Christ at His Coming (I Peter 1:7)
3. To bring glory to God (John 11:2-4)
4. To prove/test the real sincerity of our Christian faith and joy (Prov 17:3; II Cor 8:2)
5. That God teaches His children to depend upon Him alone (II Cor 1:9)
6. God to use them to share the Gospel (Phil 1:12, I Peter 3:15)
7. Future comfort of others (II Cor 1:4)
8. To be corrected by Him (Job 5:17; Prov 3:11,12)
9. That God teaches us His Law (Psalm 94:12, 119:71)
10. That God might pour His Spirit upon us (I Peter 4:14)
11. That God might give us the Kingdom of Heaven (Matt 5:10,11)
12. That we might be partakers of His holiness (Heb 12:4-11)

Quotes
➢ "If evil were not made to appear attractive, there would be no such thing as temptation."--Billy Graham
➢ "To be tempted is not to sin; the strongest attacks are made on the strongest forts"—DL Moody

43. Encouragement and Compassion

We have this huge contradiction--how important it is that people feel encouraged, that being encouraged is one of the best things that can ever happen to us how much is written (and commanded) in Scripture about the importance and power of encouragement. Encouraging one another is the main biblical reason why we attend church (Heb 10:25)! YET, so few people feel encouraged and so few people offer encouragement to others and, in fact, much of what is said between one person and another borders more being discouraging than encouraging!

The lack of encouragement in our society is an epidemic. When was the last time that someone offered you encouragement? When was the last time that_you_offered encouragement? We are fallen human beings! We tend to discourage more than encourage either directly through words or actions or indirectly by not saying or doing anything. We concentrate on others' weaknesses and faults rather than their strengths. We tend to want to tear others down rather than build up.

Encourage means to inspire with confidence; to stimulate to action by assisting and supporting; to make another feel special, to transmit trust, to challenge another to be the best he or she can be. The Greek word for encourage means to help, to comfort, to set free so that a person can move forward and realize his or her potential. God has commanded His people through the Scriptures to encourage one another: Encourage/encouragement is mentioned 63 times in Scripture: Read and discuss these four--Rom 14:19; 1 Thess 5:11; Heb. 3:13, Heb 10-24-25.

Who is the example of encouragement in the Bible? Acts 4:36-37..........Barnabas, "Bar - Naba", son of consolation/encouragement "wios paraklaseos". Read and discuss the following Scriptures that demonstrate Barnabas being an encourager—Acts 9:26-27, 11:22-23, 13:50-52, 15:36-40.

Are you an encourager? Do you want to become a greater encourager? Criticism, condemnation, sarcasm, humiliation, hostility, pity, ridicule, shame - come so naturally to our lips. But how about encouragement? Do you encourage your children or grandchildren? Your spouse? Your friends? Your neighbors? Your brothers and sisters in Christ here at church?

Three Kinds of Words (1)
1. Nothing words--Matt 12:36; Eph 5:6; I Tim 6:20.
2. Negative words--Prov 15:1;18:21;13:3; James 3:8. One negative word can hurt for a lifetime.
3. Nice words--Prov 12:25; 15:23; 16:24. Read Eph 4:29 If you are ready to utter an acerbic, spiteful or cutting comment, according to the Bible, we should ask: "Is it building up or tearing down?" "Am I giving grace in this remark?"

Words of Encouragement
- Should be intentional. Barnabas stepped in to support Paul. The apostles weren't eager to believe that Saul was now a believer. But here came Barnabas. The text says that he "took him and brought him to the apostles" and "declared" to them. Where would the church be today without Barnabas' intentional encouragement and advocacy of Paul?
- Should be timely and on the mark—Prov 25:11
- Should not be withheld. When someone does something good in your eyes, simply tell them. It will make a world of difference to that individual. Discouragement may come more so by the lack of saying anything to someone who deserves your praise. We especially need to encourage people when they are very young and when they are very old. We also can encourage others, if not directly, then indirectly by praising a member of their family. What parent is not encouraged when he or she hears something nice about their child?

As Christians, Jesus calls each of us to witness, by His grace, to the powerful effect that encouragement can have in others, as we read in the life of Barnabas. An individual is never more Christlike than when full of compassion and offer encouragement for those who are down, needy, discouraged, forgotten. Encouragement is oxygen to the soul! Some of the greatest success stories of history have followed a word of encouragement or an act of confidence by a loved one or a trusting friend. Is it possible for you today to think of one, preferably more than one, person to whom you could encourage today? And don't stop with just doing something today. Be a consistent encourager.

Self-Encouragement
1. Stop looking downward--start looking upward—Psalm 42:5. Discouragement is one of the greatest hindrances to the Christian life. We Christians too often dwell on the dark and dreary rather than the bright and sunny side of life. We look downward (at the negative) and get depressed. What gets us depressed? Aging, children growing up, failures, dreams that didn't come true, feeling worthless, feeling unloved and unwanted, feeling you haven't accomplished anything, financial problems, health problems, others?
2. Start looking upward—Psalm 121:1-2. Here is where we see truth in the Lord's statement about becoming like little children. They are light-hearted and carefree. They trust their parents implicitly for their needs.
3. Stop looking inward--start looking outward—II Cor 5:15. Christians who are depressed are really dealing with self-centeredness. Because nearly everyone can find something wrong with themselves, depression and misery can easily occur. Start looking outward. God loves you. Ask Him to forgive, cleanse, and fill you with His love. (Quote Phil. 4:6-7). The very best way to get out of depression is to lose yourself in service for God and others. How? You have God-given talents (Ask spouses to share with one another what they are). Develop them. Use them. This will enable you to look outward; be rewarded in this life and win eternal rewards in the world to come.
4. Stop looking backward--start looking forward—Phil 3:13. Many Christians become depressed because they look almost exclusively to past accomplishments (theirs and their children). They lack vision for the future and fail to advance God's kingdom on earth. Start looking forward even when results are slow coming in. If you are faithful, God will send the increase in His own time and way (I Cor 3:7). Start looking forward. You can do something for God and others. Examples? A smile, a touch, a kind word, a prayer, a note, little can be much when God is in it. Look forward always with anticipation and hope. The best is yet to come. Our heavenly home with no sorrow, suffering or separation is waiting for us.

Quotes
➤ "Kind words can be short and easy, but their echoes are truly endless"--Mother Teresa
➤ "One of the highest of human duties is the duty of encouragement. It is easy to laugh at others' ideals; it is easy to pour cold water on their enthusiasm; it is easy to discourage others. The world is full of discouragers. We have a Christian duty to encourage one another. Many a time a word of praise or thanks or appreciation or cheer has kept a man on his feet. Blessed is the man who speaks such a word."—William Barclay
➤ "He who believes in Me......out of his heart will flow rivers of living water" (John 7:38). A river reaches places where its source never knows. God rarely allows a person to see how great a blessing he/she is to others. God will use your encouraging words to act as a river, sooner or later reaching its goal being a blessing to others" Ostwald Chambers, Sept 6 devotional).

44. Money

The Bible has a lot to say about money. There are over 800 verses in the Bible that speak about money. Greg Laurie says that 15 percent of everything Jesus ever taught was on the topic of money and possessions, more than His teachings on heaven and hell combined.

Money is always a major topic that consumes our thoughts and fears as we struggle to pay bills, save, give, invest, and deal with unexpected costs. The majority of Americans live paycheck to paycheck. Various sources estimate that the majority of Americans have little or no savings. The #1 reason for marital problems is money problems. The majority of people do not know how to manage their money and money mismanagement causes people to get into enormous debt. Consumer costs keep skyrocketing (gasoline, food, insurance, taxes, credit card interest, etc). The current economic crisis we are seeing is direct result of too many people unable to pay for home mortgages and billions of dollars loaned to people who couldn't repay. A recent statistic states that 1 in 6 Americans owe more on their house than the house is now worth. Greed, materialism, hoarding, and selfishness are caused by the love and pursuit of money.

Main Teachings About Money
- Jesus' summary about money is found in Matthew 6:24 where He clearly stated that we either serve God or we serve mammon (money, riches, greed). When we allow (give priority to) money, riches, and materialism to dominate our lives, we for sure choke God's word right out of our lives.
- What He stated in Luke 16:11 says that money is a test of our true stewardship before God and what He will give us to do.
- He desires for us to save first before buying what we then can afford—Luke 14:28. See also Prov 21:20
- Be content with what you have so that you do not become materialistic—Heb 13:5; Ps 37:7,1; Prov 23:4-5; Phil 4:12-13
- You cannot love the Lord and money equally—Luke 16:13; Matt 6:19-21
- Money doesn't last—James 1:9-11, 5:1-5
- Money can easily change you for the worst—I Tim 6:8-10; Jer 9:23-24
- The Bible has much to say about materialism and hoarding--Luke 12:15-21, 16:19-31; Ps 49:16-19; Eccl 5:10-15; Prov 11:4,28
- Eagerness to get rich can hurt you—Prov 28:20; Rev 3:17-19
- The Bible gives some investment advice--Luke 16:9-12; I Tim 6:17-19; Luke 12:29-34. Prov 13:22 says that we should leave an inheritance to our children and grandchildren.
- Some Scripture seem to promise wealth (Prov 15:6, Prov 10:22; I Thess 2:5; II Cor 2:17; I Tim 6:5-9), but consider the context. For example, Proverbs are principles of wisdom, not necessarily promises.

The Six Laws of Money (1)
1. God is the real owner of money.
God owns it all, because He made it all. That includes all the money in every pocket, purse, bank account or investment account anywhere on planet earth. It's a hard or harsh truth, but it's reality: you own zero money. You were born broke; you will die broke too in the fact that you'll leave it all behind. You are a custodian, a manager, a steward of God's property, God's money. Psalm 24:1; 50:10-11; Hag 2:8; Job 1:21; I Tim 6:7.

2. God is the ultimate source and giver of money.
Wherever you get income is only a medium for getting the money from God to you. You get money normally through work. But for you to be able to work for money, you need life, health and strength, and every bit of that comes from God--Deut 8:18; Prov 10:22; Eccl 5:19; Acts 17:28.

3. Money is a powerful force.

Besides God, money is perhaps the second most powerful force in the universe. Money can become a god, an idol - either the love of it or the lack of it. Only a minority of the human race have learned the skill to surf the financial waters and waves. Sadly, most human beings swim against the tide of currency. That's why the masses are often left poor. Prov 10:15; 18:11; Matt 6:24.

4. Know the warning label that comes with money.

There is nothing wrong with money as there is nothing wrong with a kitchen knife. It just depends on whose hand it's in. Money simply takes on the morals, ethics, or character of the person handling it. The primary warning about money has to do with greed or covetousness, which can lead to "the love of money...the root of all kinds of evil". Never fall in love with money; it's only a tool for getting things done. In other words, money is like a slave that you own, a slave that can do whatever you want. But don't be fool; the monetary slave can take over if the master is absent-minded, careless, carefree, undisciplined or irresponsible with money. Job 1:21a; Eccl 6:12-13,15; Prov 11:28; 23:4-5; 28:20,22; Matt 6:19-21; I Tim 6:6-10.

5. Money does not contain or bring happiness

In this life, happiness is only found in God through Jesus, through a personal relationship with Christ. Don't base your contentment on money. Never measure your happiness by the amount of money you have or don't have. If you are miserable, no amount of money will change that. Many rich people are depressed and many commit suicide! On the other hand, some of the happiest souls on earth have little or no money. I Tim 6:6-8; Phil 4:11-13.

6. You will give an account to God for how you handle money.

Since God is the Owner and you are His manager, it only makes sense that He must require from you a report of your financial stewardship. You will report to The Master concerning everything you ever did with money. Did you use money to indulge yourself, to engage in evil, to tempt others to do evil, to promote evil, to take advantage of people, to manipulate others, to show off? Or did you use money to provide for your family, to give, and to help the poor and needy or those who help meet the needs of the less fortunate in our world? Matt 25:14-30; Luke 19:11-27; Rom 14:12; II Cor 5:10.

Questions

1. Can you give up your money if you believed God wanted you to? Mark 10:21-27,31; Acts 2:44-45, Acts 4:32-35; Luke 14:33, 16:9-12
2. Is money preventing you from bearing fruit? Mark 4:18-19; Luke 8:14, Luke 9:25
3. What does the Bible say about a Christian going into debt? Rom 13:8; Ps 37:21; Prov 22:7.
4. Can a person be a Christian and wealthy? Prov 8:18, 13:21, 21:21; Psalm 128:1-4
5. Is money the root of all evil? I Tim 6:9-10; Prov 23:4-5; Heb 13:5
6. Will God hold you accountable at the last judgment for the way you used your money? Psalm 24:1; Matt25:14-30; Rev 20:12). See next study on Stewardship.
7. Is the tithe the standard of Christian giving for us today, or was it just the standard for Old Testament Israel? Matt 5:17-19; Rom 4:12; Mal 3:8-11; Prov 3:9-10; Luke 6:38,
8. How much is enough for the Christian? II Cor 9:7; I Tim 6:17-18
9. Why give away what we earn? Rom 12:1; II Cor 8:8-9; Matt 25:31-46; Luke 12:33.
10. To whom should we give? I John 3:16-17; Deut 10:18-19; James 1:27; Rom 12:13; II Cor 9:7-14; I Tim 5:17-18; Phil 4:15-19; I Tim 5:4,8,16; Rom 13:6-7; Rom 12:20.

Quotes

➢ "Money is an article that may be used as a universal passport everywhere except heaven and as a universal provider for everything except happiness"—Wall Street Journal
➢ "The real measure of your wealth is how much you'd be worth if you lost all your money."—Unknown
➢ "If you want to feel rich, just count the things you have that money can't buy." - Proverb
➢ "Don't tell me where your priorities are. Show me where you spend your money and I'll tell you what they are". - James W. Frick

45. Stewardship

When people hear or see the word "stewardship" they think of money and giving to the church. Stewardship is much more than money and giving. The New Testament word for stewardship is "oikonomas" where "oikos" means "house and "nomos" means "law".   Biblically a steward was one to whose care was committed the management of the household (Gen 43:19; Luke 16:1). A steward in the Bible also has been applied to ministers (I Cor 4:1) and to Christians (I Peter 4:10). A biblical world view of stewardship can be defined as the use of God-given resources for the accomplishment of God-given objectives. The central essence of biblical world view stewardship is managing everything God brings into the believers life in a manner that honors God and impacts eternity. (Wikipedia Theology).

Stewardship of Time, Talent, and Treasure (1)
Stewardship involves the use of our time, talents, and treasure. Stewardship of time means careful distribution of our time spent at work, at home and with the Lord, balancing our physical, emotional and spiritual lives. Stewardship of talent means nurturing, developing and using the God-given abilities and characteristics that help to define "who we are" as individual human persons. Stewardship of treasure means the proper care and use of all the things we possess. Time, talent and treasure are all gifts from God and Christians are to care for and share these gifts with others.

- What is required of stewards? I Cor 4:1-2
- What are you doing to "make the most of your time"? Eph 5:15-17
- What did Moses pray for and why? Psalm 90:12
- What work has God given all believers to do? Matt 28:19-20; II Tim 4:5; Eph 4:11-12; Phil 1:27 and 4:9,12,13 What specific changes do you need to make to accomplish God's work?
- How could you apply Col 3:23-24 to the use of your talents, spiritual gift, and abilities?
- Are you building up the body of Christ? Eph 4:11-13
- As a good steward, what should you do? I Peter 4:10; Matt 25:14-30
- What is the precious possession of a person? Prov 12:27 How are you showing it?
- What should your attitude be toward serving the Lord? Rom 12:11
- How should believers use their money? Luke 16:9-12
- What are you instructed to do with your riches? I Tim 6:17-19
- What is the criterion for giving? I Cor 16:2 What is your personal criterion?
- List a principle from each verse from II Cor 8:2-5 as to how these Corinthian Christians gave
- What stewardship principle is taught in II Cor 9:6-7?
- What stewardship principles taught in Matt 6:19-24 and Acts 20:35?

Five dimensions of stewardship
Thomas L. Are (2) suggested that there are five dimensions of stewardship as a Christian lifestyle:
1. Worship—review study 2
2. Study—review study 8
3. Service—review study 41
4. Giving—this study
5. Loving—review studies 19 and 35

Giving (3)
Why do we give?
- Our main duty is to glorify God (I Cor 10:31). One way we do that is by good stewardship, reflected, in part, by our attitude toward money, meaning that we are to build His kingdom through support of His mission of reaching the world for Jesus Christ (Matt 28:18-20).
- We give out of gratitude for the blessing we have already received because of Christ.
- Stewardship requires us to give our time, talent & treasures to help others in need.

- We will give an account of ourselves and be judged according to our works which are what we have done with our time, talent and money (Rom 14:10-12, II Cor 5:10).

What are our barriers to giving?

- Materialism: we are under intense peer and societal pressure to increase our standard of living… build bigger houses (barns, as in the parable of the rich fool, the only man in scripture who Jesus calls "fool" to his face--Luke 12:13-21)
- Selfishness / Disobedience: we are commanded to love others as ourselves (Gal 5:14) and specifically commanded to care for the poor (Prov 19:17; Matt 25:31-46; James 2:13-17).
- Lack of knowledge about Biblical teaching regarding giving (Mal 3:8-10; Mark 10:21)

How do we decide how much to give?

- As stewards of God's resources, every financial decision is a spiritual one (Matt 6:1-4)
- When I spend money, I am acting as God's money manager. How would God want me to spend or invest his money? (II Cor 8:11-14)
- Realizing that we will one day give an account of our stewardship, we should be both sacrificial and strategic in our giving. (II Cor 9:6-7)
- When we give sacrificially, we give a little of our selfishness away and thus surrender more to Christ. When we give strategically, we are maximizing the return on His money.

How much are we supposed to give?

- Tithing is an Old Testament requirement.
- Even though it is an Old Testament command, would Jesus expect less of us lavished by His grace than of those under the yoke of the Law?
- New Testament teaches to give ourselves as a living sacrifice. (Romans 12:1-2)
- Realizing that all resources are God's and I am a steward of His resources, how much would God expect us to give? (Luke 6:38, Luke 14:33)

What steps can we take to increase our standard of giving?

- Start by tithing
- If young, minimize increases in your standard of living as your income increases.
- If older, consider lowering your standard of living.
- Think in terms of how God would want me to spend His money…do I need a bigger barn or nicer car? Ask yourself, how much is enough? (Luke 12:15-17a, 19b-21, 33)
- When planning your estate, ask how much will my children really need?

To whom should we give?

- Your church
- Ministries pursuing the Great Commission (evangelism)
- Ministries pursuing the Great Commandment. Love others and especially those less fortunate, both Christians and non-Christians you know are hurting because of circumstances/ emergencies beyond their control. (Luke 3:8-11)
- Ministries that are effective, legitimate, credible, documented.
- Ask, "would the Lord want me to give to this person/organization/cause"? (Prov 19:17)

Quotes

- "We make a living by what we get---we make a life by what we give"—Unknown
- "No person was ever honored for what he received, but a reward of what he gave."— Coolidge
- "God judges what we give by what we keep."—George Mueller
- "I have never met an unhappy giver."—George Adams
- "The world is full of two kinds of people, the givers and the takers. The takers eat well, but the givers sleep well."—Modern Maturity

46. Prayer/Meditation/Fasting (1-3)

Like most topics in this study series on Enriching Christian Doctrine and Character, two pages are woefully insufficient to capture all the main teachings about prayer. There may be more books written about prayer than any other Biblical topic. The latest book, and perhaps the best one I've ever read about prayer is Philip Yancey's Prayer: Does It Make Any Difference?, Zondervan, 2006.

The main purposes of prayer are to honor the name of God, to bring His kingdom to earth, starting with you and me, and to conform to His will (Matt 6:9-10). We pray not only to ask for God's help and answers, but, more importantly, to refocus ourselves in our circumstances to see what God wishes us to see. Prayer recognizes the reality of God in our lives (Ps 46:10). Through prayer we establish a relationship with God through Jesus Christ. During prayer we ask God for things and thank Him. During meditation God speaks to us, not only through our listening but also through our study of His word.

The disciples asked Jesus to teach them to pray in Luke 11:1-4, the only record of the disciples asking Jesus to teach them anything. They saw how vital prayer was to Jesus. We are to pray everyday (in fact, all the time) because that is what our Lord did.

Types of Prayer
- Jesus' prayers—John 17; Matt 26,; Luke 11
- "Arrow" prayers—Mark 9:24; Luke 18:13b; Luke 22:42b, I Thess 5:17
- Private prayers—Matt 6:6
- Prayers focused on specific topics/needs—see below

Prayer of Worship and Meditation
- Praising God   I Thess 5:16; Rev 19:6-7
  - o **P**repare   Matt 6:6
  - o **R**emember   Ps 77
  - o **A**dore   Ps 8,9,18,33
  - o **I**magination   Matt 19:13-15
  - o **S**ing   Col 3:16
  - o **E**xpress   Rev 2:4
- Meditation/Inner Listening   Ps 62:5-6; Josh 1:8; Rom 8:26

Prayer of Confession and Repentance
- Hindrances to answered prayer
  - o Unconfessed sin   Isa 59:2; Ps 66:18
  - o Family problems   I Pet 3:7; Matt 5:23-24
  - o Wrong motives   James 4:2-3
  - o Doubt   James 1:6-8
- Name the specific sins that need forgiveness--I John 1:9; Ps 139:23-24
- Move the sins the block God's channel of blessing--Gal 6:7; Matt 6:14-15

Prayer of Faith
- Memorize the key verses about faith   Heb 11:1,6
- God fights our battles   II Chron 20:15
- Faith is believing before receiving   Heb 11:6; Mark 9:22-23; Matt 21:22
- God's answers to our prayers
  - o Yes   Ps 37:4-5; Matt 7:7-11
  - o No   James 4:3
  - o Wait   Hab 2:3; Isa 40:31

Praying for Others
- Our loved ones .... Gen 18:16-23
- Christian leaders/others in the church ... Ps 23; I Tim 1:13,18,19; I Tim 2:11-16; Jam 5:13-16
- Our nation and our leaders .... II Chron 7:14
- Missionaries .... Rom 12:10-13
- Non-Christians .... I Tim 2:1-4
- Those who persecute you .... Matt 5:44

Praying for Yourself
- God's willingness to give .... Rom 8:32; Phil 4:19
- Have faith that He hears .... I John 5:14-15
- Live in accordance to His will .... Ps 84:11-12
- The example of Jonah .... Book of Jonah

Picture Your Prayers As Being Answered
- Ask expectantly .... Jer 33:3
- Ask believing in His answer(s) .... Matt 21:22
- Ask according to God's will .... I John 5:14-15
- Ask in Jesus' Name .... John 14:14
- God's promises always come true .... Mark 11:24

Prayer of Thanksgiving
- Continually give thanks .... Heb 13:15
- Thankful for everything in life .... Eph 5:18-20
- It is God's will to be thankful .... I Thess 5:18
- For His answers .... Phil 4:6-7

Close in the Name of Jesus
- He sympathizes with us when we pray ... Heb 5:1-2, 4:15
- He supplies all of our needs .... John 1:17, 16:23-27
- He saves us .... Heb 7:23-26
- He is seated in heaven .... Heb 8:1-2, 10:19-25

Fasting (4)
In the same section of Scripture that Jesus emphasized prayer (Matt 6:5-15), He also emphasized fasting (Matt 6:16-18) and giving (Matt 6:2-4). He stated here that we should fast in a way not to be noticed by others. There are many purposes for fasting--strengthening prayer (Ezra 8:23), seeking God's guidance (Acts 14:23), expressing grief (II Sam 1:11-12), seeking protection (Ezra 8:21-23), expressing repentance (Joel 2:12), humbling ourselves (Ps 35:13), expressing concern for the work of God (Dan 9:3), ministering to the needs of others (Isa 58:6-7), overcoming temptation (Matt 4:1-11), and expressing love and worshipping God (Luke 2:37; Zech 7:5)

Quotes
➢ "Prayer is not an easy way of getting what we want, but the only way of becoming what God wants us to be"—Student Kennedy
➢ "Daily prayer is the gymnasium of the soul"—Unknown
➢ "I have so much to do today that I must set aside more time than usual to pray"—Martin Luther
➢ "If I wish to humble anyone, I would ask him about his prayer life"—Unknown
➢ "Prayer is a shield to the soul, a sacrifice to God, and a scourge for Satan"—Unknown
➢ "Prayer is the key of the morning and the bolt of the night"--Unknown

47. Purity and Integrity

Purity

Purity is the condition of being pure and has many definitions, e.g. freedom from foreign matter (pure water), cleanness, freedom from guilt or defilement of sin, innocence, chastity, freedom from any sinister or improper motives or view, and so forth. Two main words for pure or purity in the Old Testament were "tahor", meaning physically and chemically pure (e.g. many references to pure gold in Ex 25) and "bar", meaning clean and clear (e.g. Ps 19:8 and 24:4). Two main words for purity in the New Testament are "katharos", meaning clean and clear (e.g. Matt 5:8; I Tim 3:9; James 1:27) and "hagnos", meaning innocent or chaste (e.g. Phil 4:8; James 3:17).

Purity in the Bible includes both ceremonial purity (e.g. Lev 12:2-8; Num 19:1-10; Lev 13:8; Lev 15) and ethical purity (Lev 20:1-21; Deut 22:20-21; Matt 5:27-30, 19:3-9, Mark 10:2-11; I Cor 5:9-13, 6:18-20 and 7:8-11.

The Word of God calls the people of God to live a pure life, and this type of life goes far beyond Christian sexual abstinence. Christians must strive for purity of spirit, mind, heart, and body. A purity quiz will help guide the individual in understanding why God calls people to live a life of that reflects His pure and gracious heart. Discuss what each of these verses teach about purity

- Psalm 19:8
- Psalm 119:9
- Prov 15:26
- Prov 20:9
- Matt 5:8
- Phil 4:8
- I Tim 1:5
- I Tim 2:22
- II Tim 1:3
- Titus 1:15
- James 3:17
- James 4:8

Meaning of "Pure in Heart" (Matt 5:8; James 4:8; Psalm 51:10) (1)

The Greek word translated "heart" in Matthew 5:8 is kardia, from which we get the word cardiac. The Bible always refers to the heart as the internal part of man--the seat of a man's personality. Predominantly it refers to the thinking processes--not the emotions. Proverbs 23:7 says, "As [a man] thinks in his heart, so is he." We can think of the word heart as referring to the will and emotions because they are influenced by the intellect.

Pure in heart in Matt 5:8 means a heart unmixed in its devotion and motives, a heart full of spiritual integrity and "singleness". Believers are to have singleness of heart with respect to their motives (Matt 6:21-24). You cannot serve two masters. All believers are to seek to have pure motives before God. "Katharos" speaks of more than a person's motives. A person may think his motives are pure and say he is religious, but if his deeds aren't in accord with God's Word, his heart isn't focused on God.

How can you have a pure heart?

1. Admit that you cannot purify your heart on your own—Prov 20:9; Jer 13:23.
2. Put your faith in God. Good works will not make a heart pure but faith can--Acts 15:9; I John 1:7; Zech 13:1
3. Read God's Word and pray—John 15:3

Matt 5:8 says that those who are pure in heart "shall see God.". The verb translated "to see" indicates an action that the pure in heart direct back upon themselves, thus the pure in heart shall continuously see God for themselves. When your heart is purified at salvation you begin living in the presence of God. You don't see Him with physical eyes but with spiritual ones. You begin to comprehend Him and become aware of His presence. Just as Moses saw God's glory (Ex. 34), the person whose heart is purified by Jesus Christ repeatedly sees the glory of God.

Integrity

Integrity means soundness, wholeness, incorruptible, honor, completeness. Honesty, holiness, even purity are synonyms for integrity. The Christian walking in integrity is not two different persons: one in the public eye, and another in private; or who lives differently on Sundays than the rest of the week. A person of integrity is not going to take advantage of others although he could. A person of integrity can be trusted. A person of integrity is not going to steal when no one is looking or is going to lie if he knew he could get away with it. Unfortunately the church has experienced too many leaders who have failed in their integrity.

What does the Bible have to say about integrity?
- Treat people fairly and honestly. (Lev 19:35-36; Deut 25:15; Prov 16:11-13)
- Keeping your word (Exo 8:28-32)
- Provides protection (Ps 25:21, Prov 2:7-8, 10:9, 11:3, 13:6)
- More valuable than riches. (Prov 28:6)
- The Lord will test and judge your integrity. (1 Chron 29:17; Ps 7:8)
- The Lord hates lies and lack of integrity. (Zech 8:16-17)
- It may be difficult to maintain your integrity. (Job 2:3, 2:9; Prov 29:10)
- Beware of bad company. (1 Cor 15:33)
- Integrity will be rewarded. (1 Kings 9:4-5, Neh 7:2, Ps 41:11-12)
- Your integrity should set an example. (Titus 2.7)

The armor of God in Ephesians 6 includes both purity and integrity (2)
The Girdle Of Truth – The Believer's Integrity (Eph 6:14a)
A soldier in Paul's day had a leather girdle that he tightened about his waist to protect his loins and carry his weapons of warfare, e.g. a sword. The belt also held his tunic together so it wouldn't be snagged. In Christian armor, it is integrity that holds everything else together. If you do not have integrity in the big and small things of your life, you are going to lose the battle. Without truth everything falls apart. Satan will come against you with lies and bring a lack of integrity into your life. Jesus is the Truth and will strengthen you with His integrity. Would people say that you are a woman or man of integrity? If not, then you cannot win the battle.

The Breastplate Of Righteousness – The Believer's Purity (Eph 6:14b)
The breastplate of a soldier was sometimes made of woven chain. Whatever the material, the purpose was the same – to cover the soldier's vital organs. For the Christian, the breastplate is righteousness. The enemy wants to attack you not only with lies, but also with impurity. He wants you to read filthy magazines, watch immoral movies, and engage in all temptations of the flesh. The bottom line is that Satan wants to get into your heart and mind. He's looking for a crack in your armor. And don't be fooled. Satan knows where that crack is. Is your heart pure before God? If not, then you cannot win the battle.

Questions
1. What does a pure life mean to you? What does a pure heart mean to you?
2. Who do you know that you would describe as a person of integrity? What sets this person apart from other people of a similar age and position?
3. What can you do to improve your purity and integrity?

Quotes
➤ "The way to preserve the peace of the church is to preserve its purity"—Matthew Henry
➤ "Live so that when your children think of fairness and integrity, they think of you"—H.J. Brown
➤ "The supreme quality for a leader is unquestionably integrity......His teachings and actions must agree with each other"—Dwight D. Eisenhower
➤ "Here's a worthy prayer request—God keep me pure in money, morals, and motives."—P. Howard

48. Wisdom and Discernment

Wisdom

Wisdom and knowledge (along with instruction and understanding) are closely linked in the Bible (e.g. Prov 1:7, 9:10; I Cor 12:8; and Eph 1:17). <u>Wisdom</u> is looking at life from God's point of view. Wisdom is associated with the fear (reverence) of the Lord. Wisdom gives one pause and asking the question 'What would Jesus do?" Wisdom is clarity of vision. Charles Swindoll said: "You look at difficulties and tests as God looks at them. You look at family life and child rearing as God looks at them. You interpret current events as God would interpret them. You focus on the long view. You see the truth even though all around you are deception and lies."

<u>Knowledge</u> is knowing God's Word and His deep truths. The firm foundation for knowledge is Jesus Christ – the Word, the Truth and the Light. A person with the gift of knowledge is often idea-oriented and will diligently search the scriptures to know and understand the truth that God will show him. He passionately seeks the truth and yearns for accuracy in his understanding. He is alert to shades of meaning and to nuances and subtleties of expression.

Someone can know what a Scripture says and understand what that Scripture means but not be wise in how to apply that Scripture to daily living. The spiritual gift of wisdom gives insight into the practical application of knowledge to daily life (Eccl 7:12). Wisdom brings knowledge to life in our lives. People with the gift of wisdom are problem solvers, decision-makers and counselors. They are looked to for advice and counsel.

The books of Job, Psalms, Proverbs, Ecclesiastes, and Song of Songs are considered wisdom literature. In the New Testament, James is considered a letter of wisdom; in fact James and Proverbs can be studied together because of how complementary they are.

Scriptures That Teach About Wisdom
- II Chron 1:11-12—God blessed Solomon because he prayed for wisdom
- Job 28:1-28—God alone knows where true wisdom is discovered
- Psalm 90:12—Quality of life is related to wisdom
- Prov 2:1-6—The pursuit of wisdom brings security and virtue
- Prov 3:13-20—Those who live by God's wisdom will enjoy life
- Prov 26:4-5—The wise know what is best in each situation
- Eccl 8:16-17—Even the wise do not know what God is doing
- Eccl 9:7-10—The wise enjoy life as God enables them
- Rom 1:18-20—We learn about God's wisdom by observing creation
- James 1:5—God promises wisdom to those who ask for it
- James 3:17—The fruit of God's wisdom

Proverbs—The Book of Wisdom
- 915 verses, each with a message of advice about life and conduct
- Main purpose—impart wisdom for everyday life
- Frequently uses similes to teach truths about wisdom
- Written mostly by King Solomon from 950 BC to 900 BC
- Chapter 1:2-5 contain what's known as the five faces of wisdom
    o Self-discipline (1:2a)
    o Understanding (1:2b)
    o Wise relationships (1:3a)
    o Planning (1:4b)
    o Learning (1:5)
- Proverbs 1:20-33 is God's final call for wisdom (1)

- o Wisdom's invitation—1:20
  - Public—for every person, not a select few (I John 2:2)
  - Pressing—a matter of saving one's soul (II Cor 5:11)
  - Patient—wisdom keeps waiting, even for the scorner (Prov 1:22)
- o Wisdom's indoctrination—1:23
  - Repentance of the sinner (23a)
  - Revelation of the Spirit (23b)
  - Reliability of the Scripture (23c)
- o Wisdom's indignation—1:24
  - Derision of the sinner (1:26)
  - Desolation of the sinner (1:27a)
  - Destruction of the sinner (1:27b)
- Best known Proverbs verses on wisdom
  - o 3:5-6
  - o 6:16-19
  - o 9:10
  - o 12:25
  - o 13:3
  - o 13:12
  - o 15:32
  - o 16:3,6
  - o 19:1
  - o 22:1
  - o 22:6
  - o 28:13

What are the benefits/manifestations of wisdom?
- Gentleness-- James 3:13
- Prudence, discretion and knowledge—Prov 8:12
- Power—Prov 8:14
- Right speech—Prov 10:31
- Humility—Prov 11:2
- Self-control—Prov 19:11

Discernment

The word discernment is found 43 times in Scripture. The gift of knowledge brings us truth and the gift of wisdom enables its application to our daily lives. God also provides members of His church with the spiritual gift of discernment. A person with the gift of discernment has the divine ability to differentiate between truth and error and to distinguish between right and wrong. Discernment recognizes the reality of God's truth and sees the light of His Word and can recognize a counterfeit a mile away. Discernment discerns spiritual sources (human, satanic or divine), personal motives (godly, carnal), distinguishes between truth and error and tests the spirits.

Biblical Teaching About Discernment
- I Kings 3:11
- Ps 119:66
- Prov 2:2-3
- I Cor 1:19
- Phil 1:9
- Col 1:9
- II Tim 2:7
- Heb 5:14

Quotes
- "The function of wisdom is to discriminate between good and evil."--Cicero
- "The art of being wise is the art of knowing what to overlook."-- William James
- "It is characteristic of wisdom not to do desperate things." --Henry David Thoreau
- "Wisdom consists of the anticipation of consequences." --Norman Cousins
- "Patience is the companion of wisdom." --St. Augustine
- "I hope our wisdom will grow with our power, and teach us, that the less we use our power the greater it will be."--Thomas Jefferson

49. Pride vs Humility

Proverbs 16:18 states "Pride goes before destruction and a haughty spirit before stumbling while 15:33b states "Before honor comes humility". These two verses capture the essence of the difference between pride and humility. Pride produces destruction and stumbling while humility produces honor (see also Prov 11:2 and 29:23). What is pride and what is humility?

Pride
Pride is the attitude of self-worship to think more highly of yourself than you ought. Pride is the basis for most if not all sin. Pride is listed as one of the three major evils of the world, along with lust and greed (I John 2:15-16). What is "boastful pride of life"? It can mean many things, among them obsessive pursuit of money and materialism.

Why does God hate pride so much (Psalm 138:6; Prov 8:13, 16:5; Mal 4:1; I Peter 5:5-7; I John 2:15-16)? Pride is self-centeredness rather than God-centeredness. Pride completely ignores God (Psalm 10:4). Pride ignores worship of God. Pride keeps people from accepting Jesus as their personal Savior and Lord. Pride refuses to recognize sin for what it is. Pride separates man from God. Pride gives us the credit for something that was not our doing but God's. Pride is giving ourselves the glory rather than giving glory to God. King Nebuchadnezzar (Dan 4:28-32) and the Pharisee in Luke 18:9-14 are two examples of prideful people and what God thought about them.

Signs of Pride (1)
1. Insecurity. Research reveals clergy as one of the most insecure of all professional groups. Insecurity is the root of many unhealthy and ungodly behaviors. It provokes us to want the lavish praise and attention of others too much. Much of pride is motivated out of one's unmet need for self-worth. Finding one's identity and security in Christ is a must to avoid pride.
2. The need to be right. The need to be right prevents one from appropriately evaluating issues as well as themselves (Gal 6:3). A person who needs to be right has an exalted investment in himself or herself and thinks that he/she knows better than others. In religious circles, the need to be right is frequently manifested through always saying 'God told me' or 'God showed me'.
3. Being argumentative. Individuals, who argue their point of view, especially to those in authority over them, believe that they are always right and that their will should prevail. It is appropriate to advocate for a point of view or position but not to do so in such a manner that you are more invested in your opinion than in arriving at a mutual understanding.
4. More invested in being heard than in hearing. When someone develops a pattern of needing others to listen to them rather than first hearing others, pride is motivating the need. The need to be heard is common among clergy who are insecure. Oftentimes, the individual does not feel loved or valued unless people "hear them out."
5. Anger. Anger is a self-justifying emotion. This means that the nature of anger is to prompt us to justify our position and blame another for the wrongdoing. Justification of self leads to denial of our own complicity or wrongdoing. The scripture warns strongly against anger (James 1:20).
6. Irritability and impatience. When we are unable to be patient with another and are irritated, it demonstrates a haughty view of self. We feel that our views, time or needs are more important than the other persons.
7. Lack of submissive attitude. Submission is the voluntary placement of oneself under the influence or authority of another. When an individual pledges their submission to another, yet is critical or argumentative of that authority, then pride is the hidden issue.
8. Not easily corrected. Ever work or live with someone who won't receive any negative or corrective feedback? This too is pride. Most of us need to work on this one as very few people, even Christian, react well to critical or negative feedback.
9. Receiving correction but not changing. insecurity and fear prevent prideful people from truly changing.
10. Needing others to take your advice. Counselors easily fall into the trap of having to have others take their advice. Advice should always be offered without strings attached. If you find yourself resenting the fact that your advice is not followed, look deeper at the motivating issues in your life.
11. Needing to proclaim your title or degrees. Many pastors are guilty of this, requiring others to refer to

them as "Pastor" or "Doctor". Demanding that others call you by title is usually a way of making you 'one up' and them 'one down'. Once again, pride is fueling the requirement.

12. <u>Being stubborn.</u> Webster's dictionary defines stubbornness as "unduly determined to exert one's own will, not easily persuaded and difficult to handle or work, resistant." The root issue of stubbornness is willfulness, which is 'I want what I want when I want it'.

13. <u>Comparisons and competition</u>. II Cor 10:12 makes it clear that comparing oneself with others is unwise. Comparison is a form of competition. Comparisons are subtle sins of heart that inwardly grieves when another is more successful or rejoices when another enters hard times. The motive of heart is pride.

<u>Humility</u>

Humility is the opposite of pride, a quality of a person who sincerely without self-denigration has a low opinion is his own self-importance (Rom 12:3). The two examples of humility--Moses (Num 12:3) and Jesus (Matt 11:29-30, Phil 2:5-8). Discuss Mic 6:8; Phil 2:3-4; Jam 4:6-10; I Pet 5:5-7.

<u>Twelve Ways To Humble Yourself (2)</u>

1. Routinely confess your sin to God. (Luke 18:9-14). All of us sin and fall short of the glory of God. However, too few of us have a routine practice of rigorous self-honesty examination. Daily review of our heart and behavior, coupled with confession to God, is an essential practice of humility.

2. Acknowledge your sin to others. (James 3:2, 5:16). Humility before God is not complete unless there is also humility before man. A true test of our willingness to humble ourselves is being willing to share with others the weaknesses we confess to God.

3. Take wrong patiently. (1 Peter 3:8-17). Patiently responding to the unjust accusations and actions of others demonstrates our strength of godly character and provides an opportunity to put on humility.

4. Actively submit to authority…the good and the bad! (1 Peter 2:18). Our culture does not value submission; rather it promotes individualism. How purposely and actively do you work on submission to those whom God has placed as authorities in your life?

5. Receive correction and feedback from others graciously. (Prov 10:17, 12:1). Look for the kernel of truth in what people offer you, even if it comes from a dubious source. Always pray, "Lord, what are you trying to show me through this?"

6. Accept a lowly place. (Prov 25:6,7). If you find yourself wanting to sit at the head table, wanting others to recognize your contribution or become offended when others are honored or chosen, then pride is present. Purpose to support others being recognized, rather than you.

7. Purposely associate with people of lower state than you. (Luke 7:36-39). Jesus was derided for socializing with the poor and those of lowly state. Our culture is very status conscious and people naturally want to socialize upward. Resist the temptation of being partial to those with status or wealth.

8. Choose to serve others. (Phil 1:1; II Cor 4:5; Matt 23:11). When we serve others, we are serving God's purposes in their lives. Doing so reduces our focus on ourselves and builds the Kingdom of God.

9. Be quick to forgive. (Matt 18: 21-35). Forgiveness is possibly one of the greatest acts of humility we can do. To forgive is to acknowledge a wrong that has been done us and also to further release our right of repayment for the wrong. Forgiveness is denial of self.

10. Cultivate a grateful heart. (1 Thess 5:18). The more we develop an attitude of gratitude for the gift of salvation and life He has given us, the truer our perspective of self. A grateful heart is a humble heart.

11. Purpose to speak well of others. (Eph 4:31-32). Saying negative things about others puts them "one down" and us "one up"…a form of pride. Speaking well of others edifies them and builds them up instead of us. Make sure, however, that what you say is not intended as flattery.

12. Treat pride as a condition that always necessitates embracing the cross. (Luke 9:23). It is our nature to be proud and it is God's nature in us that brings humility. Committing to a lifestyle of daily dying to self and living through Him is the foundation for true humility.

<u>Quotes</u>

➤ "As soon as you think of yourself as humble, such a thought proves that you are not"—Unknown
➤ "God has humbled Himself, but man is still proud"—Augustine
➤ "Humility is something we should pray for, yet never thank God that we have"—MR DeHaan
➤ "Nothing sets a person so much out of reach of the devil as humility"—Jonathan Edwards

50. Death and Dying

Practically every human being is afraid of death and/or the process of dying (Job 18:14; Ps 55:4-5). Even if someone claims to have no fear, that may be true, but at one time or another that person has experienced the fear of death. Sincere Christians, because of their faith in the claims of the Bible that life does not end at death, but we go to spend eternal life with God in heaven, may not be afraid of death anymore, but likely are afraid of the process of dying, especially since most deaths involve the experience of pain in the process. As Erwin Lutzner states, "Denial, anger, fear, and helpless resignation erupt in the souls of those who face death. No matter that death is common to the human race, each person must face this ultimate ignominy individually. No one can endure the moment for us. Family and friends can walk only as far as the curtain; the dying one must disappear behind the veil alone."

How do we prepare for our own death? We prepare for education, business, career, marriage, retirement, so much else, but most people do not prepare for their own death. It is easy to think of others having to keep this appointment with death, but difficult for us personally to remember and prepare for our own appointment with death.

The Bible says over 500 times that we are not to be afraid. There is no shame to be afraid and all of us are afraid from time to time. Even Jesus experienced fear before His arrest (Luke 22:44; Matt 26:39). However, the Bible clearly teaches that the only fear that we should have is to fear God with all of our hearts. If we do that there is nothing else to be afraid of, even dying and death. Jesus took away the fear of death for those who trust Him. One of the main reasons He came to earth and to die for our sins was to help His followers overcome the fear of death.

Biblical View of Death
Biblically, death means separation between two things:
- Physical death—separation between body and soul—Gen 3:17-19; Eccl 12:7; Phil 1:23.
- Spiritual or eternal death—separation between man and God—Gen 2:17; Isa 59:1-2; Luke 15:24; John 5:24; John 11:25; Rom 6:23; Eph 2:12-13; Rev 20:14-15.

There are other Biblical deaths (second death-- Rev 21:8; 22:14-15, dead to sin—Rom 6:2, marriage dissolved by death—I Cor 7:39, but these are not covered in this study)

Billy Graham and Erwin Lutzner's Teaching About Death
Billy Graham's ministry has always focused on the reality of death, but, more importantly, the good news about life after death. Here are some highlights from his book, Peace With God (1)
- All of life is but a preparation for death—I Sam 20:3; Ps 89:48; Heb 9:27
- The Bible says that we are immortal souls—John 6:51; II Tim 1:10
- Our soul will live forever in one of two places—Matt 10:28
  - o Scripture very clear that there is a Hell for every person who willingly and knowingly rejects Jesus Christ and Savior and Lord—Matt 13:41-42, 49-50; Matt 25:41; II Thess 1:8-9; Rev 20:14-15, 21:8
  - o What Scripture says about heaven—John 14:2; I Cor 5:1; II Cor 5:8; Matt 19:29; 25:34; Ps 48:2; Rev 22

Erwin Lutzer addresses most of the questions we have about death and dying (2).
- Biblical descriptions of death
  - o A departure (Luke 9:31; John 13:36; Phil 1:23)
  - o A restful sleep (Job 3:17; Dan 12:2; I Thess 4:14; Luke 8:52; John 11:11; I Cor 15:51; Acts 7:59; Rev 14:13)
  - o A return to dust (Gen 3:19; Eccl 12:7)
  - o A collapsing tent (II Cor 5:1)
  - o A sailing ship (Phil 1:23; Heb 6:19-20)
  - o A permanent home (John 14:2-3; II Cor 5:6-8)

o Good grief (I Cor 15:55; Heb 5:7; Acts 8:2; Romans 12:15)
- For Christians, what can you really expect one minute after you die?
    o One minute after you die, you will either be enjoying a personal welcome from Christ or catching your first glimpse of gloom as you have never known it.
    o Jesus told the thief on the cross that when he died he would be with Christ "in paradise" (Luke 23:43).
    o Paul said that the moment we die, we will be with the Lord (II Cor 5:8)
    o Personal knowledge continues—Luke 16:23-26; I Cor 13:12.
    o Personal love continues--the rich man was concerned about his brothers.
    o Personal feelings continue--Psalm 16:11; Rev 6:9-10.
    o Personal activities continue
- What kind of body do the saints have in heaven now? Discuss II Cor 5:1. Also, note the Transfiguration story and the rich man story.
- Questions about heaven and eternal life
    o What will our resurrection body be like? I Cor 15:42-44; Luke 24:39; and I John 3:2.
    o What about the death of infants? Will they be infants forever?
    o We think of death as our enemy. In what ways is death our friend?
    o What is your permanent home like? Rev 21:1-2, 16, 11-21
    o What will be your job description in heaven?
        - Worship of God--Rev 19:5-6
        - Service to the Lord--Rev 22:3-4
    o What will be absent in heaven that is now present on earth? Rev 21:1-4, 23, 27
- A lesson in how to die--Jesus Christ
    o He died with the right attitude (Matt 26:42; John 17:5)
    o He died at the right time (John 7:30; John 13:1-4)
    o He died in the right way (John 21:18-19)
    o He died for the right purpose (John 17:11; John 19:30)
    o He died with the right commitment (Luke 23:46)
- What does God require of you if you want assurance that one minute after you die you will be in heaven? The message of salvation--John 3:3; John 11:25; Acts 4:12; Rom 8:38-39; Eph 2:8-9; Heb 2:14-15; Rev 14:13.

Quotes

➤ "People have not learned to live who have not learned to die"—Jim Elliott
➤ "Now, I know that someday I am going to come to what some people will say is the end of this life. They will probably put me in a box and roll me right down here in front of the church, and some people will gather around, and a few people will cry. But I have told them not to do that because I don't want them to cry. I want them to begin the service with the Doxology and end with the Hallelujah chorus, because I am not going to be there, and I am not going to be dead. I will be more alive than I have ever been in my life, and I will be looking down upon you poor people who are still in the land of dying and have not yet joined me in the land of the living. And I will be alive forevermore, in greater health and vitality and joy than ever, ever, I or anyone has known before."—D. James Kennedy (who died 9-5-07)
➤ "The big question is not, 'What can I still do in the years that I have left to live?', but 'How can I prepare myself for my death so that my life can continue to bear fruit in the generations that will follow me?'" —Henri Nouwen
➤ "In order to keep us from becoming too attached to earth, God allows us to feel a significant amount of discontent and dissatisfaction in life—longings that will never be fulfilled on this side of eternity. We're not completely happy here because we're not supposed to be! You will not be in heaven two seconds before you cry out, 'Why did I place so much importance on things that were so temporary?'" —Rick Warren

51. Boldness and Courage

The word **"courage"** has no exact expression in Hebrew. There are five uses of words that are translated as "courage" in the Bible. The main Hebrew word is "chazaq" ("to show oneself strong") (II Sam 10:12; I Chron 19:13; Ps 27:14; 31:24). Also "amats", "to be alert" (physically and mentally), "to be agile," "quick," "energetic" (Deut 31:6,7,23; Josh 1:6,9,18; 10:25; I Chron 22:13; 28:20). The main Greek words for courage are either "tharseo (tharsos)" meaning "good cheer", "comfort", "boldness" (Matt 9:2, 14:27, Mark 6:50; John 16:33) or "euthameo" meaning "in fine spirit" (Acts 27:22, 27:25, 28:15). Courage is also used to mean confidence or assurance in speech (Acts 4:12, 29, 31), virtue, moral excellence, manliness, valor (II Peter 1:3, 5; Phil 4:3), the courage of one's convictions (II Chron 15:8), and fearlessness (Heb 13:6).

The word **"boldness"** is used in the New Testament (Greek: "parresia", meaning confidence, fearlessness, freedom of speech). This was one of the results of discipleship (Acts 4:13,29,31; Eph 3:12; Phil 1:20; I Tim 3:13; I John 4:17). Paul uses the word in the sense of plainness in II Cor 3:12. In Heb 10:19 and I John 2:28; 4:17, it has the sense of freeness resulting from confidence. In Philem 1:8, the reference is to the authority which Paul claims in this case.

Courage is strength in the face of danger or opposition. The Bible contains many examples of courage. Three times Moses charged all Israel and Joshua with the same words "Be strong and courageous" (Deut. 31:6, 7, 23). God charged Joshua three times with the same words (Joshua 1:6, 7, 9). God knew how much they needed courage to face giants in the walled cities in the land promised to them. The command points to the premium that God places on the obedience of faith to His covenant promises and commands. Courage must be guided by the Word of God to achieve success. Courage is the manifestation of faith that God will not leave nor forsake His people.

Our model for courage is Jesus. Fixing our eyes on Jesus, we are to "run with perseverance the race marked out for us" (Heb 12:1-3). Remember that Jesus Himself has marked out the course we must run--approaching God boldly in prayer, courageously seeking "to be pleasing to Him", fearlessly speaking the Word of God, standing strong "against the devil's schemes", justly and courageously pointing out sin in the church, and supporting courageous discipline.

Some specific examples of Biblical courage (1)
Exodus 1:15-22; Esther 3:2; 4:13-16 Daniel 3:16-18
Courageous people risk their lives to do what is right. Hebrew midwives helped women give birth and cared for the baby until the mother was stronger. When Pharaoh ordered the midwives to kill the Hebrew baby boys, he was asking the wrong group of people. Midwives were committed to helping babies be born, not to killing them. These women showed great courage and love for God by risking their lives to disobey Pharaoh's command. Against Pharaoh's orders, the midwives spared the Hebrew babies. Their faith in God gave them the courage to take a stand for what they knew was right. In this situation, disobeying the authority was proper. God does not expect us to obey those in authority when they ask us to disobey him or his Word. Esther and Mordecai and Shadrach, Meshach, and Abednego are some of the people who took a bold stand for what was right. Whole nations can be caught up in immorality (racial hatred, slavery, prison cruelty); thus following the majority or the authority is not always right. Whenever we are ordered to disobey God's Word, "we must obey God rather than men" (Acts 5:29).

Luke 23:50-56
Courageous people risk their reputations to do what is right. Joseph of Arimathea was a wealthy and honored member of the Jewish Council. He was also a secret disciple of Jesus (John 19:38).

The disciples who had publicly followed Jesus fled, but Joseph boldly took a stand that could cost him dearly. He cared enough about Jesus to ask for his body so he could give it a proper burial.

Acts 4:23-31

Courageous people are bold in representing Christ. Boldness is not reckless impulsiveness. Boldness requires courage to press through our fears and do what we know is right. How can we be more bold? Like the disciples, we need to pray with others for that courage. To gain boldness, you can (1) pray for the power of the Holy Spirit to give you courage, (2) look for opportunities in your family and neighborhood to talk about Christ, (3) realize that rejection, social discomfort, and embarrassment are not persecution, and (4) start where you are by being bolder in small ways.

Deuteronomy 33:26-29

Courage grows as we trust God. Moses' song declares that God is our refuge, our only true security. How often we entrust our lives to other things—perhaps money, career, a noble cause, or a lifelong dream. But our only true refuge is the eternal God, who always holds out his arms to catch us when the shaky supports that we trust collapse and we fall. No storm can destroy us when we take refuge in him. Those without God, however, must forever be cautious. One mistake may wipe them out. Living for God in this world may look like risky business. But it is the godless who are on shaky ground. Because God is our refuge, we can dare to be bold.

John 16:17-33

Courage grows from the presence of Christ Jesus summed up all he had told them this night, tying together themes from 14:27-29; 16:1-4; and 16:9-11. With these words he told his disciples to take courage. In spite of the inevitable struggles they would face, they would not be alone. Jesus does not abandon us to our struggles either. If we remember that the ultimate victory has already been won, we can claim the peace of Christ in the most troublesome times.

Three characteristics to believe and act as Christians with courage (2)

1. Conviction—essentially the state of being free from doubt. It is the tenacious trust that God really is working all things for good in our behalf (Rom 8:28). It is certainty that we do not face dangers and opposition by ourselves (Heb 13:5). Real courage is not only overcoming fear, but also willingness to stay the course, to keep our eyes focused on Jesus.
2. Commitment—a willingness to act on our convictions, to be accountable (Luke 9:62). Com-mitment comes as we count the cost and choose by an act of the will to follow through. Be careful not to keep your commitment private. It must be lived out in the community of others.
3. Confidence—assurance that we are not alone. The cross is forever a symbol of hope. It is God's personal commitment to be with us and for us (Heb 6:19).

Questions

1. Is courage a characteristic commonly attributed to Christians? Why or why not?
2. II Chron 15 shows Asa, the God-fearing king, mustering courage to remove the idols from the land. What idols might need to be removed from your own life? Why might it take courage to remove those idols?
3. What situations do you presently face that might inspire fear? What kinds of fear? How can you draw courage from what you know of the Lord?

Quotes

➢ "Courage is doing what you are afraid to do. There can be no courage unless you're scared"—Eddie Rickenbacker
➢ "Courage is fear that has said its prayers"—Unknown
➢ "It takes more courage to face grins than to face guns"—Unknown
➢ "You will never do anything in this world without courage. It is the greatest quality of the mind next to honor."—James Allen

52. Contentment and Peace

Contentment

Being content and at peace are the most treasured, wonderful, and blessed feelings to experience in all of life. Yet, contentment and peace are not natural human emotions. Without contentment we don't have peace of heart and mind. We live in a society that is full of discontent. People gravitate toward being discontented about what they have (or rather don't have), what they look like, what job they have, and in whatever circumstances they live. People who complain all the time are discontented and lack peace. It seems that people complain about everything, especially our jobs, other people, even our church.

Contentment is the opposite of coveting. Not to covet is one of the Ten Commandments (Exo 20:13-17, see also Eccl 5:10-11; Prov 1:19). Therefore, being content with what you have is being obedient to this commandment. We are commanded to be content, but most people are not content and, therefore, breaking a major commandment of God. God puts covetousness (discontentment) as a sin equal to that of murder because discontentment is questioning the goodness and provision of God. Discontentment is a very serious sin that permeates our nature and our society.

The best verse on contentment on the Bible is Phil 4:11. Contentment is a quality that is learned through life's experiences, it is not a natural characteristic of humankind and certainly our culture easily causes discontentment. Learning contentment is not via any external experience such as success, achievement, wealth, materialism, etc.

David Curtis preached a wonderful sermon on contentment (1):

1. **Contentment comes from trusting God even when life seems unfair—Eph 1:11.** We can trust God because He rules the universe and all that happens in it. God has a plan, and He is working His plan (Phil 1:6). God's plan may not always seem fair to us, but then where did we ever get the idea that life is supposed to be fair (John 16:33)? The seed of contentment is planted through trusting God to take care of us when treated unfairly. Think of the example of Joseph (Gen 50:20). Discontentment results from trying to control everything in your life and becoming frustrated when you cannot. Learn to trust the Lord.

2. **Contentment is developed by being certain of God when life is uncertain—II Cor 11:23-29.** We know that not knowing is worse than knowing (eg waiting for results of medical tests). There will be times in all of our lives that consist of uncertainty. It was only by going through days and nights of uncertainty that Paul discovered that God knows how to take care of His children in uncertain times.

3. **Contentment comes when we learn to be satisfied with the basics of life—Phil 4:11; I Tim 6:6-11.** None of us lack these things, but are you content? Our culture loves to produce discontentment via advertising, and if we listen to advertising we are never content. We need to meditate on the words of Jesus until we are convinced of their truthfulness. We must learn the truth of Luke 3:14, 12:15, and Heb 13:5 if we are ever going to be content.

4. **Contentment is perpetuated by being concerned for the well being of others—I Tim 6:6; Matt 22:36-40; Phil 2:3-4.** If you live only for yourself, you will never be content. Contentment begins to be a reality when you have more concern about how it is with others than about how it is with you. If we are not putting others first, we are not Godly, and if we are not Godly, we will never be content. Contentment is derived in this life from what we give to others, not in what we gain for ourselves.

Questions

1. Do you know anyone who is truly content? What have they learned?
2. How content are you? What does it take for you to be content?

Peace

The OT Hebrew word for peace is <u>shalom</u> meaning soundness, health, prosperity and well-being ((Ps 29:11, 35:37; 73:3, Isa 26:3). Shalom is used as a friendly greeting, asking about one's health and in farewells (Gen 29:6, 43:23, 27; Judg 6:23). The NT Greek word for peace is <u>eirene</u> that has the same meaning as shalom (Luke 2:14; Rom 5:1; Mark 9:50; John 14:27).

Romans 5:1 says it all....."Therefore, having been justified by faith, we have peace with God through our Lord Jesus Christ". Billy Graham published a famous book <u>Peace With God</u> that elaborates on what peace with God really means in the life of a Christian.

The following verses contain profound truths about the meaning and application of peace. Write out what each verse teaches to you:

- Ps 119:165_____
- Prov 3:13-17_____
- Isa 26:3_____
- John 14:27_____
- John 16:33_____
- Rom 8:6_____
- Rom 14:17-19_____
- Gal 5:22-23_____
- Eph 2:14-18_____
- Phil 4:6-7_____
- Col 3:15_____
- Heb 12:14_____

R.A. Torrey (2) wrote that Enoch's walk with God (Gen 5:24) describes the secret of abiding peace (as well as abounding joy and abundant victory). Walking with God:
- means to live in God's presence and in conscious communion with Him.
- gives abounding joy (Ps 16:11)
- gives a great sense of security and of abiding peace (Ps 16:8)
- gives us fearless courage (Isa 41:10; Ps 27:1)
- results in beauty of character (II Cor 3:18)
- results in eminent usefulness because He is pleased with us (Heb 11:5)

Questions
1. Are you at perfect peace with your life? What must you do to have God's peace?
2. How would you define the peace of God? What Bible verse means the most to you?

Quotes
➢ "It may be all right to be content with what you have; never with what you are" – BC Forbes
➢ The secret of contentment is knowing how to enjoy what you have and be able to lose all desire for things beyond your reach" – Lin Yutang
➢ "Christianity means certainty, security, and peace of mind" – Billy Graham
➢ "Lack of peace means that you are outside the will of God" – Unknown
➢ "Peace rules your life when Christ rules your mind" – Unknown
➢ "Peace is the deliberate adjustment of my life to the will of God" – Unknown

References

1. God the Father
    1. http://www.lifetalk.net/lifequest/study/father.html
    2. Billy Graham, God's Seven Wonders, <u>Decision</u>, July-Aug, 1986

2. Worship
    1. http://home.att.net/~nathan.wilson/worshipwordstudy.htm
    2. http://ezinearticles.com/?What-Does-it-Mean-to-Worship-God?-(Part-3)&id=281032
    3. http://www.elite.net/~ebedyah/PastorsSite/foundations/foundstudy9.htm.

3. Seeking God
    1. <u>http://www.dianedew.com/seekgod.htm</u>
    2. Gary Henry, Westside Church of Christ, Indianapolis, IN

4. The Will of God
    1. Leslie Weatherhead, <u>The Will of God</u>, Abingdon Press, 1944.
    2. Charles Swindoll, <u>The Mystery of God's Will</u>, Word Publishing, 1999.

5. Grace and Mercy
    1. Edward Fudge, <u>The Grace of God</u>, Presidential Press, 1971.

6. Creation
    1. Tom Holladay and Kay Warren, <u>Foundations</u>, Zondervan, 2003, pp 214-216
    2. Tom Holladay and Kay Warren, <u>Foundations</u>, Zondervan, 2003, pp 230-242

7. Faith and Faithfulness
    1. Jim Gerrish, <u>Bridges For Peace</u>, Jerusalem, 1995
    2. http://www.churchisraelforum.com/faith_and_faithfulness.htm

8. The Truth of Scripture
    1. John MacArthur, <u>How To Study The Bible</u>, Word of Grace, 1985

9. Covenants
    1. (http://www.gotquestions.org/bible-covenants.html) (1,2)
    2. Scofield, http://focusonjerusalem.com/basicsonbiblicalcovenants.html
    3. http://www.ldolphin.org/Maincov.html   <u>The Faithfulness of God</u>   A sermon delivered by the late Ray C. Stedman on February 23, 1992.

10. Fear and Reverence
    1. www.bible.com.
    2. www.atruechurch.info/fearofGod.com

11. Hope and Security
    1. Charles Swindoll, <u>Hope Again</u>, Word Publishing, 1996.

12. Protection and Guidance
    1. (http://www.sundayschoolresources.com/bdprotection.htm

13. Heaven, Hell, and Eternity
    1. "A Letter From Hell", www.godtube.com

14. Sin
    1. www.Bible.org
    2. http://parentalguide.com/Documents/Bible_Studies/Sin_list_part_6.htm

15. The Life of Jesus
    1. www.Topverses.com
    2. http://www.jesuscentral.com/

16. The Cross
    1. http://www.christian-faith.com/forjesus/the-meaning-of-the-cross

17. Salvation
    1. R.A. Torrey, Decision, Oct, 1999, 26-27

18. Confession and Repentance
    1. http://orthodoxwiki.org/Repentance.
    2. Nancy Missler King's High Way http://www.khouse.org/articles/2002/420/
    3. http://www.kencollins.com/pray-25.htm
    4. The Book of Common Prayer, page 360

19. Forgivenss
    1. http://www.talkjesus.com/daily-devotionals/11915-gods-forgiveness-eternal-freedom.html
    2. http://www.lifetv.org/Web_HTML/html/Commentary%20folder/Forgiveness.htm

20. Purpose of Life
    1. Rick Warren, Purpose-Driven Life, Zondervan, 2002

21. Victory
    1. http://www.raystedman.org/1corinthians/3607.html
    2. http://blogs.chron.com/thinkingchristian/2006/06/victory.html

22. Discipleship
    1. MJA notes from sermon given by Dr. Adrian Rogers sometime in 1978-1979.
    2. Oswald Chambers, My Utmost for His Highest, July 2 devotional

23. Righteousness and Holiness
    1. Bill Burkett, http://www.actsion.com/holright.htm
    2. http://pastorway.blogspot.com/2006/09/true-righteousness-and-holiness.html

24. Suffering and Persecution
    1. Jane McWhorter, Let This Cup Pass, Quality Pubs, 1978.
    2. http://www.itpartners.org/articles/Toward%20a%20Theology%20of%20Suffering.pdf

25. Backsliding
    1. http://www.biblestudyplanet.com/s19.htm; Alban Douglas lessons
    2. http://christianity.about.com/od/practicaltools/ht/avoidbackslide.htm

26. Prophecy and the Second Coming
    1. http://www3.telus.net/thegoodnews/propheticsigns.htm
    2. http://www.allaboutgod.com/the-second-coming.htm

27. Soul and Spirit
    1. http://www.gotquestions.org/soul-spirit.html
    2. http://www.wcg.org/lit/spiritual/soulspirit.htm

28. The Work of the Holy Spirit
    1. http://www.realtime.net/~wdoud/topics/holyspirit.html

29. Witnessing/Soul Winning
    1. http://mb-soft.com/believe/txw/witness.htm
    2. William Bright, "The Christian and Witnessing", in <u>Ten Basic Steps Toward Christian Maturity</u>, Campus Crusade for Christ, 1965

30. Mind and Thoughts
    1. http://lifestrategies.thingseternal.com/growinthefaith/thoughtlife.html
    2. www.intouch.org
    3. Keith Drury, http://www.indwes.edu/Tuesday

31. Conscience
    1. http://atschool.eduweb.co.uk/sbs777/snotes/note0303.html
    2. John McArthur, <u>The Vanishing Conscience</u>, Word Pub, 1994.
    3. http://atschool.eduweb.co.uk/sbs777/snotes/note0303.html
    4. MacArthur, <u>http://www.gty.org/Resources/Articles/23</u>

32. Spiritual Gifts
    1. John Piper, http://www.soundofgrace.com/piper81/031581m.htm
    2. Bill Gothard, Seminar on <u>Basic Life Principles</u>, Institute in Basic Youth Conflicts, 1979

33. Power
    1. http://www.bible-history.com/isbe/P/POWER/
    2. http://sewhttkr.home.comcast.net/~sewhttkr/stories/38_godspowr.htm
    3. Charles Swindoll,<u> Come Before Winter</u>, Multnomah Press, 1985, p. 135

34. Joy
    1. John MacArthur, http://www.biblebb.com/files/MAC/sg50-1.htm
    2. James Orr, Orr, ed, <u>Definition for 'JOY'</u>, International Standard Bible Encyclopedia, 1915, http://www.bible-history.com/isbe/J/JOY/

35. Love
    1. http://www.biblestudyguide.org/articles/walk-love.htm

36. Sanctification
    1. Bible-knowledge.com
    2. Alban Douglas, <u>One Hundred Bible Lessons</u>, Daniels, 1966
    3. Lehman Strauss http://www.bible.org/page.php?page_id=361

37. Patience
    1. http://www.bellaonline.com/articles/art35881.asp
    2. http://cgg.org/index.cfm/fuseaction/Library.sr/CT/PERSONAL/k/266/The-Fruit-of-Spirit-Patience.htm
    3. RL Skelton,<u> Decision</u>, July-Aug, 1990, pp 31-33)
    4. www.coping.org

38. Gentleness/Meekness
    1. www.associatedcontent.com/article/264793/fruit_of_the_spirit_gentleness.html
    2. http://my.homewithgod.com/mkcathy/studies/fruit_meek.html

39. Self-Control
    1. www.covenantseminary.edu/resource

40. Fellowship and the Church
    1. Rick Warren, <u>Purpose Driven Life</u>, Zondervan, 2002, pp 138-143

41. Calling and Service
    1. http://www.ucgstp.org/lit/bsc/bsc7/godcalling.htm
    2. http://www.crossroad.to/HisWord/verses/topics/call.htm
    3. http://trbc.org/new/sermons.php?url=20001008.html
    4. http://www.biblestudysite.org/37.htm

42. Tests and Temptations
    1. Larry Wolfe, http://www.btmi.org/outlines/12purposes.html

43. Encouragement and Compassion
    1. Walt Wiley, Maranatha sermon, Muskegon, MI, Sept 2005

44. Money
    1. http://ezinearticles.com/?What-the-Bible-Says-About-Money,-Part-1&id=1240990

45. Stewardship
    1. http://www.geocities.com/campuschristians_tx/studies/steward.html
    2. Thomas Are, <u>My Gospel of Stewardship</u>, Inst Church Revival, 1977
    3. http://www.hopeccf.org/learn/bible.htm

46. Prayer/Meditation/Fasting
    1. Jill Briscoe, <u>Hush, Hush, It's Time to Pray—But How?</u>, Zondervan, 1978
    2. Hope McDonald, <u>Discovering How to Pray</u>, Zondervan, 1976
    3. Rosalind Rinker, <u>Prayer: Conversing with God</u>, Zondervan, 1959
    4. DS Whitney, <u>Spiritual Disciplines for the Christian Life</u>, Navpress, 1991, pp. 151-17

47. Purity and Integrity
    1. John MacArthur, http://www.biblebb.com/files/mac/sg2203.htm
    2. Adrian Rogers, http://www.lwf.org/site/News2?abbr=for_&page=NewsArticle&id=5451&news_iv_ctrl=1261

48. Wisdom and Discernment
    1. Adrian Rogers, <u>God's Way To Health, Wealth, and Wisdom</u>, Broadman, 1987

49. Pride vs Humility
    1. http://www.bible.com/bibleanswers_result.php?id=223
    2. Alfred Ellis, http://www.propheciesofrevelation.org/faqs42.php

50. Death and Dying
    1. Billy Graham, <u>Peace with God</u>, Spire Books, 1953
    2. Erwin Lutzer, <u>One Minute After You Die</u>, Moody Press, 1997

51. Boldness and Courage
    1. http://aogo.org/Courage.html
    2. Loy Reed, <u>Decision</u>, 1994

52. Contentment and Peace
    1. http://www.bereanbiblechurch.org/transcripts/topical/contentment.htm
    2. R.A. Torrey, "The Secret of Abiding Peace" <u>Decision</u>, Nov 1989